Nicolas Joseph Laforet

Why Men Do Not Believe

Or, The principal causes of infidelity

Nicolas Joseph Laforet
Why Men Do Not Believe
Or, The principal causes of infidelity

ISBN/EAN: 9783744747974

Printed in Europe, USA, Canada, Australia, Japan

Cover: Foto ©Thomas Meinert / pixelio.de

More available books at **www.hansebooks.com**

WHY MEN DO NOT BELIEVE;

OR, THE

PRINCIPAL CAUSES OF INFIDELITY.

WHY MEN DO NOT BELIEVE;

OR, THE

PRINCIPAL CAUSES OF INFIDELITY.

BY

N. J. LAFORET,

PRELATE PROTONOTARY APOST. AD INSTAR PARTICIPANTIUM, RECTOR OF
THE CATHOLIC UNIVERSITY OF LOUVAIN.

NEW YORK:
THE CATHOLIC PUBLICATION SOCIETY,
126 NASSAU STREET.
—
1869.

INTRODUCTION

TO THE

English Translation

OF

"POURQUOI L'ON NE CROIT PAS."

T will doubtless be asked why this pamphlet has been singled out from among the numerous productions of Catholic apologists, and presented to the public in an English dress. The numerous and highly self-satisfied class of obstructives will not fail to question the opportunity and necessity of such a publication. But we are fain to believe that its very subject-matter, as indicated in the title, will be an ample justification of our choice to all reflecting minds capable of discerning and appreciating the tendencies of contemporary thought. The nature and drift of these tendencies can no longer be a matter of mere opinion with those who dare to look facts in the face. The most undeniable characteristic of the age in which we live, even in this country which owes so much to the conservative common-sense instincts of the English mind, is scepticism, unbelief, not only in the exclusive claims of this or that form of positive and dogmatic Christianity, but in any supernatural communication

whatever of God to man. We hear on every side the divorce of modern educated thought from belief in the supernatural order proclaimed with a portentous unanimity, so much the more noteworthy as the feelings elicited by this acknowledgment are divergent. By some, this movement of the age is hailed as the dawn of an epoch of universal enlightenment; as the supreme effort of the human mind to shake off the trammels of its long infancy; while to others it harbinges a storm which will work sad havoc in those institutions hitherto regarded as essential to the well-being and permanence of society. Thus the problem handled in the following pages by the light of the data of history and psychological observation is one which may well claim the attention of thoughtful minds. But, further, many of our brethren in the faith whose lot is cast in English-speaking communities, must have felt at times the need of an impartial and intelligent answer to the question which heads these pages—"Why Men do not Believe." They look around them and see men whose conscientious earnestness and estimable qualities of mind and heart they freely acknowledge, banded together in frenzied hate, or supercilious contempt of those principles and institutions which claim, by so many titles, the allegiance of their reason and deepest feelings; and their distressed piety, and, mayhap, their tottering faith, demand, "How can such things be?" Without ascribing to the author the merit he himself repudiates, of having exhausted a problem which requires for its full solution an insight, not only into the shortcomings and imperfections of purely mental processes, but into the dark and impenetrable depths of the human heart and conscience, we may safely promise those who will devote a few leisure hours to this essay an intellectual treat. The position of the author, who for many years was Professor of the Theological Faculty of the time-honored Catholic University of Louvain, his clear-headed accuracy, his candor and liberality, the conspicuous absence from these pages of any bitterness of feeling, the judicial calm wherewith he handles topics so well fitted by their associations and actuality to disturb it, are a sufficient earnest of his competency to deal with this question, and claim for him the attention of all thoughtful, fair-minded men of every school or party. The rapid and alarming advance of Rationalism in the high places of the Established Church, and in the national universities, heretofore the homes of orthodox teaching, dispense us from commenting on the relation indicated by the writer between the religious movement of the sixteenth century and that of our day. Public facts, unlike theories, though never so logically plausible, may not be ignored, nor will we weaken their witness to the views set forth by the learned professor by reflections on current events, which sufficiently tell their own tale. We conclude by joining with the author in the pious hope that this translation may be no less successful than the original it reproduces, in strengthening the convictions of those who believe, and in enabling such as have gone astray to retrace their steps to the Temple of Truth, whose Founder and Builder is God made manifest in the flesh.

X. Y. Z.

PREFACE.

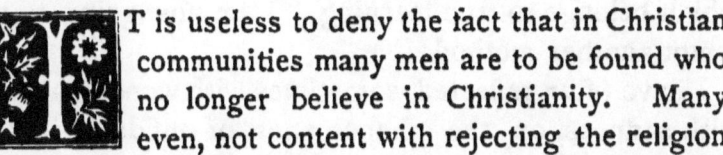T is useless to deny the fact that in Christian communities many men are to be found who no longer believe in Christianity. Many even, not content with rejecting the religion of Jesus Christ, go on to deny God; or if they do not deny him in express terms, their idea of him is radically false, and they seek to place upon the altar of the living God, the Creator of heaven and earth, a philosophical idol, ten thousand times more vain than the idols of wood and stone to which pagan nations offered incense. Whence comes this infidelity? According to those who pride themselves on being philosophers or critics, the denial of Christianity, or even of a personal and living God, is dictated by science and reason; it is the natural and legitimate fruit of intellectual progress; rationalists, spiritualists, materialists, atheists, pantheists, sceptics of every kind, all alike appeal to science and reason to justify their disbelief or their doubts in the eyes of the public, and even apparently to their own conscience. I willingly bear this testimony to learned unbelievers of every shade, that they can shelter their infidelity under the finest and noblest pretexts. I have no intention here to examine or discuss those scientific and philosophical pretexts which they call decisive and unanswer-

able reasons. This I have done elsewhere,* and Catholic writers continue to do so daily with the authority which belongs to true learning. I am now going to attempt another method.

I have often reflected, sometimes with wonder, always with sadness, on the phenomenon of infidelity in the midst of the light of Christianity. I have frequently asked myself, in the sincerity of my heart, why so many men—many of whom are noble-minded, serious, learned—reject the teaching of the Catholic Church—the organ and representative of our Lord Jesus Christ upon earth—why certain minds, rather than submit to the authority of the Church, will descend to a total denial of the moral and religious order, and even to universal doubt. In this fact there is certainly matter for a psychological and moral study of high importance and melancholy interest. I know very well that in the eyes of infidels this fact appears the simplest and most natural thing in the world; I know that they affect to place their infidelity under the direct and exclusive patronage of science and philosophy; but I am convinced that science and philosophy are in no way interested in the hostile or indifferent attitude which they assume toward the Christian faith. Christians have always possessed, and still, thank God, possess, as large a measure of science and philosophy as infidels. Infidelity depends on other causes. What these causes are I propose now to make the object of my inquiry. I cannot hope to bring to light all the real causes of infidelity; there are some which necessarily escape the eye of the observer, how-

---

*In a work entitled *Les Dogmes Catholiques, exposés, prouvés et vengés des attaques de l'hérésie et de l'incrédulité.*

ever attentive he may be; there are mysteries in the depths of the human soul which the eye of God alone can penetrate. But it is easy for any one who has had an opportunity of closely observing believers and unbelievers, and of studying their history, to recognize the principal and ordinary causes of infidelity.

This work will be divided into two parts, one historical, the other critical. In the first part, after a few words on the preaching of Jesus Christ, and the opposite effects produced by it, we shall mark, by a few examples, the principal phases of the twofold history of the Christian faith, and of unbelief in the bosom of Christianity; this history will afford us valuable lessons; it will show us how men become, how they remain, and how they cease to be Christians. We shall see, by the experience of eighteen centuries of the human mind, whether the source of infidelity can possibly be the development of reason, and the progress of intelligence. In the second part, relying on the lessons of history and on psychological and moral observation, we shall seek to unfold the real causes of religious unbelief. We shall begin by defining the nature of faith, and the nature of infidelity; we shall then analyze the principal forms of contemporary infidelity, and we shall seek to distinguish the diverse and often complex conditions of the soul, to which they attach themselves, or by which they are produced.

We trust that God will make use of these pages, humble though they be, to confirm some souls in the happy possession of the Faith, and to rescue others from the corroding bitterness of doubt, or from the gloomy, icy void of unbelief, leading them back to the bright and sweet repose which Christian faith alone can give.

LOUVAIN, January 1, 1864.

PREFACE TO THE SECOND EDITION.

HIS book has already produced consoling fruits; God has used it as his instrument to bring back many wandering souls to Christian Faith and practice.

The Sovereign Pontiff had foretold this result in a letter addressed to the author a few weeks after the publication of this work. We give a translation of this letter, which was published by the *Revue Catholique* of Louvain in the May number of 1864:

LETTER OF THE SOVEREIGN PONTIFF.

ILLUSTRIOUS AND REVEREND SIR:

To the more considerable works which you have already published, you have added one which, though small in size, will, as its title promises, prove of the greatest utility. For, as in the art of healing the body its diseases are treated with the greatest ease and security when their true cause is known, so may the maladies of the soul be best and most effectually resisted and cured when their origin has been ascertained. As the plague of infidelity, which is the principal evil of our day, proceeds either from corruption of heart, or from the languor of religious feeling, or from the madness of pride, to discover such causes and to bring them to light, by tearing from them the veil under which they disguise their shameful deformity, will assuredly be a powerful aid to the minds of men to reject these errors, and to give them also a free access to the truth. Therefore our most Holy Father, Pope Pius IX., although the numberless cares which press upon him have not yet permitted him to read the book which you have presented to him, especially approves its design, and has charged me to return to you his thanks, and to assure you from him that he foresees most abundant fruit from the labor which you have undertaken, and, as a pledge of that success, to convey to you his Apostolic Benediction, which he gives you with the tenderest affection.

Having had the pleasure of fulfilling this agreeable task, I offer you also the expression of my particular respect and esteem, and pray God to bestow all his favors upon you.

Your most humble and devoted servant,

FRANCISCUS MERCURELLI,

ROME, April 16, 1864.   (Latin Secretary to His Holiness.)

TABLE OF CONTENTS.

PART I.

CHAP. I.—The preaching of Jesus Christ—Some believe our Lord's words, others reject them—Whence arises this difference of attitude and conduct 17

CHAP. II.—The manner in which the Christian Faith took possession of the world—An example of the conversion of learned men and philosophers—St. Justin 26

CHAP. III.—Decisive triumph of Christianity in the Roman world—End of the persecutions—Constellation of great men in the bosom of the Church of the fourth century . . 44

CHAP. IV.—St. Augustine—His unbelief and his return to the Faith 49

§ I.—How Augustine loses the Faith—He rapidly descends all the steps of unbelief—He falls into materialism and scepticism 50

§ II.—Augustine's return to the Faith—He passes through an intellectual and moral crisis before his conversion . 59

CHAP. V.—The Christian Faith of the Middle Ages—It is paramount in society and governs men of high intellect as well as the common people—Was this a blind Faith? 72

CHAP. VI.—Protestantism and reason 87

§ I.—Primitive Protestantism—Age of Leo X.—The real doctrines of Luther and his accomplices—Denial of reason and liberty—War declared against science—Immediate effects of these doctrines 90

§ II.—The negative principle of Protestantism, or the rejection of authority in matters of religion—Fanaticism and rationalism the twofold fruit of this principle . . . 105

CHAP. VII.—Modern infidelity—Infidelity prevails first in England, afterward in France and Germany—Poverty of the infidel philosophy of the eighteenth century—Theological infidelity in Germany 111

CHAP. VIII.—The principal forms of contemporary infidelity—Materialism—Pantheism—Sophistry and scepticism—Spiritual rationalism 124

PART II.

CHAP. I.—What Faith is 139

CHAP. II.—Infidelity: In what it consists 157

CHAP. III.—It is impossible to attribute the infidelity of the present day to the progress of reason and science—Numerous conversions among learned men—Augustin Thierry and Maine de Biran 163

CHAP. IV.—Real causes of infidelity—First cause: Ignorance of religion 181

CHAP. V.—Causes of religious ignorance—It is often voluntary, culpable ignorance—Levity and moral indifference of most infidels 192

CHAP. VI.—Materialism—On what it rests—The soul materialized—How the soul arrives at this state, and what moral treatment must be followed to raise it from this degradation 200

CHAP. VII.—Scepticism—In what it consists—Different causes of scepticism 217

CHAP. VIII.—Corruption of the understanding—Sophistry and its victims 226

CHAP. IX.—Unbelievers who admit the fundamental principles of natural religion—Causes of their unbelief 232

CHAP. X.—Recapitulation of the causes of infidelity—How a young man may become an infidel 243

WHY MEN DO NOT BELIEVE;

OR, THE

PRINCIPAL CAUSES OF INFIDELITY.

PART I.

CHAPTER I.

The preaching of Jesus Christ—Some believe our Lord's words, others reject them—Whence arises this difference of attitude and conduct.

THE parable of Lazarus and the rich man, recorded by St. Luke, contains a passage which, at the first glance, claims especial attention. A rich voluptuary, without compassion for the sufferings of the poor, dies, and is condemned to the torments of hell; whilst Lazarus, who had lived in extreme poverty and affliction, is carried by Angels to the bosom of Abraham, the father of the faithful. The rich man, seeing himself hopelessly lost, implores Abraham to send Lazarus upon earth, to enlighten and un-deceive his brethren, who, like himself, were living in opulence and preparing for themselves a similar eternity of woe. Abraham thus answers this unhappy victim of wealth: "Your brethren have Moses and the Prophets; let them hear them." "No, father Abraham," replies this miserable reprobate; "but if one went to them from the dead, they will do penance." Abraham said unto him, "If they hear not Moses and the Prophets, neither will they believe if one rise again from the dead."* The history of the preaching of the Gospel, the whole history of Christianity, bears unanswerable testimony to the profound truth of the judgment which our Lord puts into the mouth of Abraham. People are apt to imagine that a striking miracle, performed under such circumstances as ought to banish doubt from any reasonable mind, must overcome opposition and silence contradiction. But this is a grave error which experience condemns. The majority of men who, knowing Jesus Christ and his Church, believe not, would not believe more readily though one went to them from the dead. This assertion admits of abundant proof.

At the commencement of our Lord's preaching St. John the Baptist sent two of his disciples to ask if he were the Messiah whom the world was looking for, and Jesus answered them: "Go and relate to

---

* St. Luke xvi. 19-31.

John what you have heard and seen: the blind see, the lame walk, the lepers are cleansed, the deaf hear, the dead rise again, the poor have the Gospel preached to them. And blessed is he that shall not be scandalized in me."* Such were the wonders daily performed by Jesus Christ; each of his steps was, so to speak, marked by a miracle; he exercised absolute sovereignty over all nature; nothing resisted his voice; he called forth the dead from the grave with the same ease with which he gave sight to the blind or calmed the angry waves. His doctrine, his life, his moral character, were equal to his power. Never man spake as he did. His lessons infinitely surpassed those of all the wise men who had preceded him; and men asked in amazement whence came this sublime wisdom to a man who had not followed the teaching of any master. What life was ever to be compared to his in dignity, in moral grandeur, in modesty, goodness, unselfishness, in devotion to duty! He presented the ideal of moral perfection to the eyes of all men.

Such is Jesus Christ as the Gospel narrative shows him to us, such as he revealed himself to the Jews when he presented himself to them as the expected Messiah, as the only Son of God, as the Word made flesh for the salvation of men.

And how was he received? What effect did this threefold and incomparable miracle of the power, the doctrine, and the life of Jesus produce upon the

* St. Matthew xi. 4-7.

Jews? We have just heard these astounding words uttered by his own lips to the disciples of John: "Blessed is he that shall not be scandalized in me." And in fact, he was and still remains a subject of scandal to the greater part of mankind. His contemporaries who saw and heard him were divided into two or three different categories with regard to him: some believed in him, others were indifferent and appeared to take no heed either of his works or his person; many pursued him with implacable hatred. What happened after the raising of Lazarus? That was a glorious miracle, manifestly attesting divine power. It was a miracle performed before the eyes of a crowd of persons who had flocked to the tomb of Lazarus. They knew that he had been dead four days; they supposed that his body already showed symptoms of decay;[*] and yet, at the command of Jesus, "Lazarus, come forth,"[†] he that had been dead rose immediately from the grave and appeared full of life. Now listen to the continuation of the Gospel narrative: "Many, therefore, of the Jews who were come to Mary and Martha, and had seen the things that Jesus did, believed in him. But some of them went to the Pharisees, and told them the things that Jesus had done. The chief priests,

---

[*] "Domine, jam fœtet, quatriduanus est enim."—Joan. xi. 39.
[†] "Voce magna clamavit: Lazare, veni foras. Et statim prodiit qui fuerat mortuus, ligatus pedes et manus institis, et facies illius sudario erat ligata. Dixit eis Jesus; solvite eum, et sinite abire."—*Ibid.* 43-44.

therefore, and the Pharisees gathered a council, and said: What do we, for this man doeth many miracles? If we let him alone so, all will believe in him, and the Romans will come and take away our place and nation."* The chief of the council, the high priest Caiphas, gave advice that Jesus should be sacrificed for the safety of the people. This advice was adopted by his colleagues, and from that moment the elders of the nation sought to put *him* to death who had restored Lazarus to life. Nor was that sufficient. Lazarus had become the object of universal curiosity, and afforded embarrassing proof of the Almighty Power of Jesus. The chief priests, therefore, determined to put Lazarus also to death.†

Thus did men who were exclusively devoted to material interests receive such a miracle as the raising the dead to life. And the same story will be repeated again and again in the course of the preaching of Christianity. To induce men to believe it is not enough for the light to shine before their eyes; before all things they must have a sincere and constant intention to keep their eyes open and to turn them in the direction of the light. The Gospel affords several instances of this moral phenomenon, which, moreover, all of us may observe in different degrees, both in ourselves and in

* Joan. xi. 45-49.
† "Cogitaverunt autem principes sacerdotum, ut et Lazarum interficerent: quia multi propter illum abibant ex Judæis, et credebant in Jesum."
—Joan. xii. 10, 11.

those around us. The understanding does not act alone; it is in great measure under the dominion of the will, which directs it and fixes its attention on those objects which are pleasing to itself. The truth of this main point of psychology, especially of moral and religious psychology, will become more evident as we proceed.

Among the eye-witnesses of the raising of Lazarus, some beheld in this miracle a proof of the divinity of Jesus Christ; but what of the rest? Many of these men, indifferent to all morality and influenced only by their levity or perhaps their cupidity, hastened to report the fact to the Pharisees, whom they knew to be the enemies of our Lord. It was impossible to deny the miracle, but they shut their eyes to the religious consequences which flowed from it; they sought to turn it to their own profit or to make use of it as an instrument of their vengeance.

The sacred historian relates, in another part of the Gospel, that the Pharisees, having seen Jesus cure a man who had a withered hand, immediately resolved on his destruction.* Everything which our Lord did irritated them; the more miracles he performed, the more proofs of his divinity he gave, the more was their hatred kindled against him; the more did their fury rage, the more eagerly did they seek to make away with him.

* Matt. xii. 13, 14.

We meet with another class of persons in the Gospel; men who did not hate Jesus Christ like the Pharisees, but who still did not believe in him; men who held aloof, some from fear of compromising themselves, others from levity of mind and indifference on matters of religion. Pilate affords us a memorable example of this culpable levity and this fatal indifference with regard to all that is of supreme importance to man. We are all familiar with the examination which our Lord underwent at the hands of this wretched judge, whose name has become a by-word for prevaricating cowardice, before he was delivered to the Jews, who clamored for his death. The Divine Victim, desirous to raise the soul of his judge above the paltry occupations and interests of a day, said to him, in the course of this examination, "I came into the world that I should give testimony to the truth; every one that is of the truth heareth my voice. And Pilate said to him: What is truth?" This question of surpassing interest was directly suggested by our Lord's language, and was about to be answered by that infallible Teacher, but Pilate did not wait for the answer. Scarcely had he put the question before he left the judgment-hall to seek the accusers of Jesus, and thought no more of inquiring for the truth.* Here is the type of excessive levity. What is truth? Men know not, and they do not care to know. For Pilate, the truth

* "Dicit ei Pilatus: Quid est veritas? Et cum hoc dixisset, iterum exivit ad Judæos."—Joan. xviii. 38.

was his rank as governor; all that he feared was to compromise his position. He saw only material interests in life; riches and glory absorbed all his thoughts; the moral world was closed to him. How should such men as he was believe in the preaching of Jesus Christ?

Our Saviour has himself described several of the moral causes which hindered many of his contemporaries from believing in him. Pride, injustice, corruption of manners, levity of mind, these, according to the testimony of the Son of God, are the chief moral obstacles which close the soul against the entrance of his word. "How can you believe," said he to the proud Pharisees, "who receive glory one from another, and the glory which is from God alone you do not seek?"* And elsewhere: "Light is come into the world, and men loved darkness rather than light, for their deeds were evil. For every one that doth evil hateth the light, and cometh not to the light, that his works may not be reproved?"† Are not these the chief moral causes of religious infidelity in every age? Jesus Christ pointed out to the Jews, who refused to receive his doctrine, that the root of unbelief is in the will rather than in the understanding: "You will not come to me," said he to them.‡ He was moved by the disdainful and hostile attitude of the chief priests in the presence of the wonderful miracles which he daily wrought, to cry out to God, Father: "I confess to thee, O

* Joan. v. 44.   † Joan. iii. 19, 20.   ‡ Joan. v. 40.

Father, Lord of heaven and earth, because thou hast hid these things from the wise and prudent, and hath revealed them to little ones."* The Word by whom the world was made voluntarily annihilated himself, as St. Paul says, in order to restore man ruined through pride : humility is the condition of belief in this God and Saviour.

Again, Our Lord, when explaining the parable of the sower, taught that the cares and riches and pleasures of this life are thorns which too often choke the seed of faith.†

Such are the lessons which the teaching of Jesus Christ presents to us on the twofold question of faith and unbelief. These lessons, which call for the consideration of every reflecting mind, are confirmed by the whole subsequent history of Christianity.

* Matt. xi. 25. † Luc. viii. 14.

CHAPTER II.

The manner in which the Christian Faith took possesstion of the world—An example of the conversion of learned men and philosophers—St. Justin.

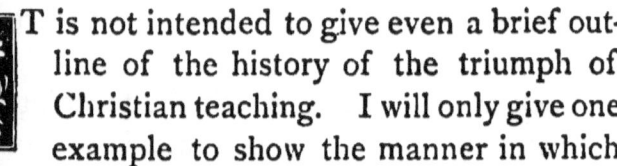T is not intended to give even a brief outline of the history of the triumph of Christian teaching. I will only give one example to show the manner in which the new faith took possession of the loftiest intellects of the pagan world.

We know how the mass of pagan society received the preachers of the Gospel. That society had become a very sink of corruption, and it defended itself with a kind of frenzy against the moral invasion which attacked all that it loved, adored, and idolized. For three centuries the blood of the disciples of Jesus Christ flowed almost without intermission. We can with difficulty understand the cruelty manifested toward them by the masters of the Roman world.

The era of public persecutions began with Nero. Tacitus, who gives the history of the first persecution, reveals in his narrative the horror with which the new religion was regarded by his fellow-countrymen.

A considerable part of Rome had been destroyed by fire, and public rumor attributed the conflagration to the orders of Nero. "To put a stop to these reports," says Tacitus, "the Emperor sought out criminals—miserable wretches who were held in abhorrence for their crimes, commonly called Christians, and exposed them to the most cruel torments. Christ, from whom they took their name, had suffered under the Procurator, Pontius Pilate,* in the reign of Tiberius, and his death had repressed for the time this execrable superstition. But the torrent soon broke forth anew, not only in Judea, where it arose, but in Rome itself, the centre where all disasters and crimes meet at last and assume increased dimension. Those who openly avowed themselves Christians were first seized, and afterward, on their deposition, vast multitudes were convicted not so much of the crime of setting fire to Rome as of hatred of the whole human race.† Derision was added to their torments; some were enveloped in the skins of wild beasts and thrown to dogs to be devoured; some were crucified;‡ the bodies of others were covered with pitch and they were made to serve as torches to give light at night. Nero gave up his own gardens

* "Auctor nominis ejus Christus, Tiberio imperitante, per procuratorem Pontium Pilatum supplicio affectus erat."
† "Igitur primum correpti qui fatebantur; deinde indicio eorum multitudo ingens, haud perinde in crimine incendii quam odio humani generis convicti sunt."
‡ St. Peter, the first Pope, was crucified.

for the spectacle, and at the same time opened the games of the circus where the emperor mingled with the people dressed as a charioteer, or taking post in the chariot races."*

Thus did the Master of the world understand the dignity of a sovereign ; thus far did a society without compassion carry its contempt for human life and its hatred of Christianity.

Tacitus condemns Christians on public report ; he knew nothing of them. One word of his, however, describes admirably the radical opposition between paganism and Christianity: This immense multitude, he says, was convicted, not so much of having set fire to Rome as of hatred of the human race. Tacitus shows clearly enough that he was convinced of the innocence of the Christians of the conflagration of Rome ; but that they were convicted of hatred of the human race is profoundly true, though in a very different sense from that intended by the Roman historian. The disciples of a God made man through love of men could not hate men ; but they did hate with a burning hatred all that was idolized by the foolish and corrupt human race of whom Tacitus speaks, and they were therefore necessarily looked upon as its mortal and irreconcilable enemies. The world owes its renovation and refreshment to this generous hatred of the religious and social ideas, the manners and customs, of a society which was rotten to the core.

* *Annal.* lib. xv. n. xliv.

The new Religion, born of the sacrifice of the Cross and founded by the Blood of Jesus Christ, could not be arrested in its course by the fury of pagan rulers. The Blood of Martyrs became the seed of Christianity. Within two centuries of the death of Jesus Christ, Tertullian, who had himself abjured the superstitions of heathenism and embraced the Christian Faith,[*] feared not to write thus to the Roman proconsuls: "We are but of yesterday, and we already fill all that belonged to you ; towns, islands, fortresses, even camps, the troops, whether tribunes or decurions, the palace, the senate, the forum : we leave you nothing but your temples."[†]

Christianity, in the first years of the preaching of the Gospel, was recruited principally from the ranks of the people, though even in the time of the Apostles a certain number of rich and learned men were received into its bosom. It had pleased the Divine Restorer of humanity to call, in the first instance, the little ones and the poor, the despised of a carnal world which adored only fortune and power. But by degrees, illustrious sages, whom the pride of knowledge had failed to intoxicate, came to swell the humble beginnings of Christian society.

Souls of a higher order, who were in some degree inflamed with the love of what was true and excellent, found themselves in a strange as well as pain-

---

[*] "De vestris fuimus ; fiunt, non nascuntur Christiani."—*Apol.* xviii.
[†] *Apol.* xxxvii. 9.

ful position amid the superstitions of idolatry. All pagan religions had two serious defects; they were neither reasonable nor moral. They were not religions in the higher acceptation of the word. And yet the human soul, if not wholly debased by vice, is naturally religious, and the mind turns instinctively to regions above the world of sense. The masses, who are not in the habit of reasoning, and in whom feeling and imagination preponderate, might perchance find sufficient aliment in the external practices and numerous festivals consecrated by mythology. Besides which they lived in a state of moral ignorance bordering on stupidity. But how could men of cultivated minds, in whom the moral sense was not totally extinct, accept the tissue of absurd and often immoral fables on which the religious worship of Greece and Rome rested? I have read most of the documents which antiquity has bequeathed to us touching Grecian philosophy, and I do not know of two philosophers who seriously believed the popular religion. It was not possible. They rarely had the courage to condemn it, and they despised the lower orders too much to seek to free their minds from the monstrous errors by which they were enslaved, especially as such a course would have been attended with danger; but, as regards themselves, they did not believe the greater part (I dare not say all) of these extravagant fictions. They were well aware that they must not seek for truth in the popular creed: they sought it in ancient traditions, in the teaching of men who had been most renowned for wisdom, in their own meditations ; but if they were able to raise themselves above the grosser errors of the multitude, they could never attain to the pure and serene profession of truth, with regard to God, with regard to man, with regard to the relations between God and man ; and many of them even fell into errors worse than the popular superstitions. How sad was the moral condition of Xenophon, of Pythagoras, Philolaus, Anaxagoras, of Socrates, Plato, Aristides, of Zeno of Cittium, of all those noble and obstinate seekers after truth who have left so honorable a trace in the history of philosophy !

Christianity is the only religion which has ever united in a common faith, equally clear, complete, and steadfast, the common people and philosophers, the ignorant and the learned. It affords a singular phenomenon in the annals of humanity.

As early as the second century of the Christian era a great number of eminent and cultivated minds had embraced the Faith of Jesus Christ. One of them, the philosopher Justin, has left us an account of his conversion. The narrative is singularly instructive. I will relate the principal facts, and we shall learn, by one memorable example, the way by which philosophers arrived at the True Faith.

Justin made a profession of philosophy, and continued to wear the philosopher's mantle even after his conversion to Christianity. He was born in Samaria either at the end of the first or beginning of the second century. He studied Greek literature with ardor, and his writings attest that he had attained a considerable degree of mental cultivation. The gross doctrines of paganism could not satisfy a serious and elevated mind such as his. The thirst after truth devoured his soul. He was prepared to seek it at all risks, and to follow it when found. He tried, in the first instance, the schools of philosophy in highest repute; he applied by turns to stoicism, to peripateticism, to pythagorism, to platonism: "Philosophy," said this noble mind, "is truly a great treasure, of great price in the eyes of God to whom it leads, and in whose sight it alone can make us acceptable."* Justin flattered himself that he should be able to obtain from the most famous masters of philosophy clear answers to those religious questions, which every soul not absolutely debased necessarily asks itself. He went from error to error. For one moment, however, he thought he had met with the object of his search. The philosophy of Plato, the purest and most elevated of the pagan systems of philosophy, seemed at first sight destined to give full satisfaction to the religious cravings of his mind; he was transported with joy at meeting with this beautiful system which promised to unveil before his eyes the realities of the world of intelligence. His pilgrim·

* *Dialogue with Tryfho*, n. 2.

ages to the schools of Pythagoras, Aristotle, and Zeno had been futile. "I resolved," he says, "to confer with the followers of Plato who are held in high repute. One of their principal teachers had just arrived in our city. I put myself in communication with him, and after long conversations I found myself daily making fresh progress. The knowledge of the world of intelligence transported me with joy: the theory of ideas gave wings to my understanding.* I fancied I had become learned in a short time, and flattered myself that I should soon arrive at the contemplation of God, which is the aim and end of Plato's philosophy."†

But there are grave omissions and important errors in Plato's teaching. Justin was some time before he perceived them. As yet he was ignorant of the new doctrine whose light was beginning to dissipate the darkness in which the highest intellects vainly struggled. He knew that Christians existed, but he probably shared the disdainful and hostile sentiments of the intellectual men of his time toward them. Still he did not believe in the monstrous and infamous crimes which the world at large imputed to them, and to which Tacitus alludes in the passage quoted above. "I also," he says, "when I was attached to Platonism, had heard of the crimes imputed to Christians; but when I saw them face death, and all that men are wont most to

* A familiar expression of Plato.
† *Dialogue with Trypho*, n. 2.

dread, without fear, I could not conceive it possible that they passed their lives in disorder and voluptuousness. How was it possible to suppose that a man who was a lover of pleasure and intemperance, a slave to the flesh and worldly delights, should court death, which would deprive him of these goods? Far from running to meet certain condemnation, would he not, on the contrary, conceal himself from the vigilance of the magistrates in order to enjoy the pleasures of life as long as possible?"*

Nothing could be simpler than this reasoning. The generous philosopher was struck by the constancy of the Martyrs; and if he did not yet ask himself whence came this heroism, his reason was at any rate free from the absurd prejudices which blinded the eyes of the multitude. Prejudice, next to the passions, is one of the greatest obstacles which the Christian Faith has encountered in every age. Let men once cast off prejudice and sincerely pursue the search after truth, and truth will not hide itself from their eyes. It was not long before Justin became a Christian. He relates himself, in the opening of his dialogue with the Jew Trypho, how he became acquainted with and embraced Christianity. He quickly passed from the school of Plato to the school of Jesus Christ.

It happened that one day, in order to be able to apply himself with greater freedom to the contemplation of the world of intellect to which the Pla-

* II. *Apol.* n. 12.

tonic philosophy had introduced him, he repaired to a solitary place near the sea-shore. Thither he was followed by an old man of venerable aspect, whose countenance bore the impression both of gravity and sweetness. Justin stopped and could not forbear expressing his astonishment at meeting any one in that solitude.* " I did not expect," said he to the old man, " to meet any one here." " I am in trouble," replied the unknown, " about some of my friends who are travelling, and I came here to see if by chance they might be visible in some point of the horizon. But what brings you to this solitude?" " As for me, I take a delight in these rambles, because, free from all distraction, I can here commune with myself at my ease; for solitude is eminently favorable to philosophy." " Ah! you are one of those who love words without troubling yourself about actions or truth, and who neglect what is practical for the sake of vain speculations." Justin thus attacked began to speak in praise of philosophy, and to extol it as the necessary source of all moral dignity. " Does philosophy necessarily confer happiness?" asked the old man. " Certainly; and philosophy alone can do so." " If nothing forbids it, explain to me what philosophy is, and what is that happiness of which it is the source." " Philosophy," replied Justin, " is the science of being, and the knowledge of truth; happiness is the re-

* Justin must have been at Ephesus or Alexandria. He lived for some time in these two cities. He afterward settled at Rome, where he founded a school.

ward of this science and of this wisdom." This is, in fact, the Platonic idea of philosophy, and it is a noble and generous idea; but it cannot be realized by the unassisted power of human reason.

The confident disciple of Plato then went on to explain briefly to his companion what was the doctrine of his master with regard to God and the soul of man. The old man, versed in the teaching of Jesus Christ, pointed out to the philosopher the weak points, the omissions, the manifest errors of this doctrine, remarkable though it be in many respects; and he particularly insisted on the absurdity of the doctrine of the metempsychosis, which Jean Reynaud, Pierre Leroux, Laurent, and certain *savants* have endeavored to resuscitate in our days in the name of progress. Justin knew not how to answer; all his philosophical illusions forsook him. His mind was in confusion, and not knowing how to calm it, he cried out in accents of despair, "To whom shall I go; where is truth to be found if not in the teaching of these men who are the oracles of philosophy?"

Justin's companion, having clearly pointed out the insufficiency of philosophy, proceeded to reassure him, and introduced him to a far higher school than that of Plato: "At a distant period of our history, long before the time of those who pass for philosophers, there lived men who were blessed, just, beloved of God; they were inspired by the Holy Spirit, and foretold future events, which have been fulfilled in our days: they are called prophets. These men alone had knowledge of the truth, and they announced it to men without weakness or fear; they were strangers to any thought of vain glory, and only taught what the Holy Spirit had given them to see and hear. Their writings still exist; whoever reads them with faith will derive from them great profit, and will be enabled to understand the beginning and end of things, and all that a philosopher ought to know. They do not proceed by way of demonstration; they are sincere witnesses of the truth, and above all demonstration: the accomplishment of what they announced compels us to believe their words. Besides, the miracles they performed placed their testimony above suspicion. They glorified God the Father, Creator of the universe, and announced to men his Son Jesus Christ, sent by him. As for you, before all things, pray that the gates of light may be opened before you; for no one can see and understand these things unless God and his Christ give him understanding."*

Prayer! Philosophy knew nothing of this mode of arriving at the knowledge of the truth. The gates of faith—faith which is the true moral and religious light—open of themselves to prayer; for God is pleased to communicate himself to the humble, and prayer, being the acknowledgment of our

* *Dialogue with Trypho*, n. 7.

insufficiency and poverty, is the expression of humility. Justin soon experienced this.

He continues thus : " When the old man had said these things and many more which I cannot relate here, he left me, recommending me to meditate on what I had heard. Since then I have not seen him. But my soul, inflamed with holy desire, longed ardently to become acquainted with the Prophets and those men who are the friends of Christ. Passing over in my mind the conversation that had taken place, I found that this was the only certain and useful philosophy. Thus and for this reason I am a philosopher." Would that all might follow the same road, so as not to wander from the doctrine of the Saviour ; for this doctrine possesses a majesty calculated to strike those who have deviated from the right path, and those who meditate on it will find in it rest full of sweetness.* Rest in a luminous and immovable certainty ; this was the end which the restless, ardent soul of the philosopher pursued. The careful reading of the Holy Scriptures, and meditation on the doctrine of Jesus Christ, soon brought him to this happy end. Scarcely had he entered this divine school than he comprehended that there were safer and more perfect masters than Pythagoras and Plato. A new world was unveiled before his eyes. He saw that from the beginning God had spoken to men by a positive revelation ; that he had afterward created a nation expressly to

* *Dialogue with Trypho*, n. 8.

preserve, develop, and preach Revealed Truth, and to announce and prepare the world for universal redemption; that in the fulness of time he had sent his own Son, the Lord Jesus, to perfect man's education and to accomplish the great work of his regeneration. What new and magnificent prospects for a mind thirsting after knowledge, and how insignificant must the schools of Greece have appeared to him beside this grand school, visibly held and governed, not by a man of genius, but by the Word of God in Person!

We, who were born and have grown up in the full light of Christianity, can with difficulty picture to ourselves the effect which this sudden transition, from the schools of Grecian philosophers to the school of the Word made flesh, produced on pagans of pure and elevated character. It was literally passing from the darkness of night to the light of day. What deep, enthusiastic joy animates the meetings of these illustrious converts! Charity kindled in their souls the fire of proselytism, and they ardently desired to bring all the unhappy victims of error to participate in the ineffable delight which they found in the Christian Faith. What deep-seated happiness, what ardent proselytism, shine forth together in that eloquent passage with which Justin, now become the apologist of the Christian religion, closes his discourse to the Greeks: "Come, O Greeks! and participate in a wisdom that is incomparable!* Instructed by a Divine Word, you will become acquainted with a King who is not subject to corruption; with heroes who have not distinguished themselves from the rest of their fellows by their crimes. The Divine Word who is our head does not desire in us strength of body, nor beauty of form, nor nobility of birth; but a pure mind established in holiness, virtuous actions by which the world may discern what King we serve. It is by the Word that a secret virtue penetrates the soul. A celestial herald! announcing peace to the soul convulsed by war! Salutary messenger! extinguishing the fire of the passions! . . . Draw near then, O Greeks! suffer yourselves to be instructed. Become such as I am, for I also have been as you now are. The Divine virtue of the doctrine and power of the Word triumphed over me. Like the skilful enchanter who draws from his lurking-place the serpent he would put to flight, the Word banishes sensual pleasures from the depths of the soul; first covetousness, from which spring the evils most to be feared, enmities, dissensions, envy, jealousy, anger, and all that resembles them. Let covetousness once be drawn from the breast, and the soul recovers peace and security. All things necessarily return to their place of origin and point of departure; therefore, when the soul is delivered from the vices

* . . . χαὶ σοριᾳ ἀπαραμιλλήτω χοἰνωνήσατε.

which make war against it, it returns of its own accord to its Creator."*

The teaching of the Word made flesh worked at once a moral and intellectual revolution in the soul. It was, according to St. Paul's words, the renovation of the whole man, *nova creatura*.

The manner in which the philosopher Justin arrived at the Christian Faith must arrest the attention of the observer. From the moment that the true idea of God, as the Creator of the world and the beginning and last end of man, took possession of his mind, he was won over to Christianity. We gather this from the narrative of his conversion, and from the general bearing of his doctrinal controversies against paganism. In spite of his wanderings among the many schools of philosophy, this noble intellect knew little of the nature of God and of his relations with the world; and the knowledge of God being the true source of the knowledge of ourselves, it followed that he had little knowledge of man; the nature of man, his origin and his end, and the path to be followed to attain that end, were so many enigmas of which the answer was hidden from him. Christian doctrine, by revealing to him the relations between God and finite creatures, gave him the key to all these problems. How could he refuse to accept the witness of Christianity with regard to mysteries of an order above human reason, when the same teaching

* *Orat. ad Græcos*, n. 5.

resolved so clearly and fully, and in a manner so conformable with reason, those important questions, the solution of which he had vainly sought in all the schools of philosophy? Besides, he comprehended that God, being the Creator and Father of man, must himself have instructed man in that which it was of supreme importance for him to know, and must have established upon earth some authority commissioned to maintain and teach the True Religion. He had now met with this authority, and to it he owed the solution of those problems which had hitherto perplexed him: how could he refuse to hear and follow its teaching? Further, when a man attains the knowledge of God, when he believes in his infinite goodness and his love for men, there is nothing in Christianity, in spite of all its marvels, to astonish him. To the grateful and enraptured soul of the philosopher, the Christian Religion appeared the most glorious, and if I may so say, the most natural, manifestation of the love of God to man.

St. Justin sealed his belief in the Christian Faith with his blood, about the year 168, after having gloriously defended it in writings which cannot be read even in our days without fervent religious feeling.*

In the second century and in the beginning of

---

* The Abbé Freppel, professor of sacred eloquence at the Sorbonne, has recently published a very complete and valuable treatise on the life of St. Justin.

The Principal Causes of Infidelity. 43

the third, we find many pagans distinguished by genius and learning following the example of the philosopher Justin, and bowing down their reason before the majesty of the Gospel. Three of them have left names of especial celebrity: Athenagoras, Tertullian, and Clement of Alexandria. We do not know the details of the conversion of these illustrious men. From this time a great number of learned writers were to be found among Christians. Besides those we have already named, it will suffice to mention Theophilus of Antioch, Melitus of Sardis, Saint Irenæus, Bishop of Lyons, Pantenus the master of Clement and first teacher of the renowned Christian school of Alexandria, Origen, Saint Hippolytus of Porto, Minutius Felix, Saint Dionysius of Alexandria, and Saint Cyprian, Bishop of Carthage. Such men as these assuredly did not believe blindly. Some of them have left remarkable works in defence of the Christian Faith. The writings of Origen on the Holy Scriptures still command the admiration of critics.

CHAPTER III.

*Decisive triumph of Christianity in the Roman world
—End of persecution—Constellation of great men
in the bosom of the Church of the fourth century.*

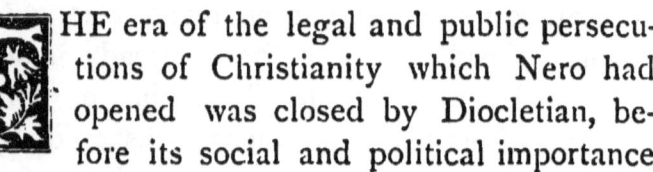HE era of the legal and public persecutions of Christianity which Nero had opened was closed by Diocletian, before its social and political importance was recognized. From Nero to Diocletian, Christianity had not ceased to extend its pacific conquests; it had invaded the whole empire, and numbered a vast multitude of disciples of every class even in Rome itself; it had penetrated the highest ranks of society; some of the noblest citizens of the empire sought refuge in its bosom. It had become, therefore, a serious matter, even on political grounds, to engage in a general persecution of the Christian Church. But Galerius Cæsar, whose cruel nature thirsted for blood, and who was a prey to all the superstitions of paganism, urged Diocletian to pursue rigorous measures. The emperor made a long resistance, but at length, after having taken the advice of a council of judges and of the heads of the army, after having consulted the Oracle of Apollo at Miletus, which declared that the presence of Christians upon earth was the cause

that only false answers were issued from the tripod, he resolved, in concert with Galerius, to annihilate Christianity. In the year 303, he published an edict, which is one of the saddest monuments of intolerance and cruelty: "All Christians, without exception, are to be stripped of their honors and dignity; no rank, no position will serve as protection against torture; all persons are at liberty to bring actions against them, but they cannot bring an action against any one, however great the injustice of which they may have to complain; churches are to be destroyed, ecclesiastical property confiscated, religious books burnt; Christians are to be allowed no liberty and no voice in public matters."* In the beginning of the year 304, the punishment of death was decreed against all who would not abjure Christianity, and from that moment the blood of Christians flowed in torrents from one end of the empire to the other, with the exception of Gaul, which was governed by Constantius Chlorus. "It is impossible," says Dr. Döllinger, "to depict the atrocious emulation of the persecutors in the invention and application of infernal tortures; the words of Lactantius are too weak to describe it when he says, 'A voice of groaning was heard over the whole earth, which from the east to the west (with the exception of Gaul) was devastated by the fury of three most ferocious

---

* Euseb. *Hist. Eccl.* lib. viii. c. 2; and Lactant. *De Mort. Persecut.* n. xiii. Patrol. ed. Migne, t. vii. col. 214.

wild beasts—Diocletian, Maximianus, and Galerius.' "* The name of Diocletian has remained attached to this persecution, which lasted about seven years, and caused frightful carnage. The pagan rulers thought they had ruined the cause of the new religion for ever, and to perpetuate the memory of their triumph they caused medals to be struck, with inscriptions of this kind: " The name of Christian is destroyed, the Christian superstition is everywhere abolished, and the worship of the gods propagated."† Fools that they were; they knew not that the religion of the Cross had been born in blood; they forgot the lesson which so many persecutions ought to have taught them, that the blood of Martyrs is the seed of Christians. At the very time that these blind representatives of a bloody power flattered themselves that they had stifled Christianity in blood, he who reigns in heaven was laughing at their shouts of triumph, was preparing their tomb, and weaving the crown which his justice, too long ignored, was about to place on the victorious head of Christianity, henceforth to be recognized as the ruler of the empire of the world.

In the year 313, Constantine and Licinius, who were the real heads of the empire, published at Milan that celebrated edict which, by placing Chris-

* *Origin of Christianity.*—Lactant. t. i. p. 178, trans. of M. Leon Boré.

† " Nomine Christianorum deleto, superstitione Christiana ubique deleta, et cultu deorum propagato."

tianity on a perfect equality with the pagan religion, gave it definitive freedom. The religion of Jesus Christ, thus set free, was able to show itself in the light of day ; and the pagans, who had just celebrated its obsequies, were struck with amazement when they beheld the innumerable multitude which professed it. Paganism was vanquished ; its day was over. Julian the Apostate might attempt its restoration, but the only result was to cover it with ridicule in the eyes of all men, and to bury it for ever under universal contempt and execration.

The fourth century is undoubtedly one of the most glorious periods in the history of the Church, especially with regard to science and learning. It is the great era of Christian literature. It was adorned by eminent men of all kinds ; St. Athanasius, Eusebius of Cæsarea, St. Basil, St. Gregory Nazianzen, St. Gregory of Nyssa, St. Cyril of Jerusalem, Didymus and St. Cyril of Alexandria, St. Epiphanius, St. John Chrysostom, Lactantius, St. Hilary of Poitiers, St. Eusebius of Vercelli, St. Ambrose, St. Jerome, St. Augustine. These were all eminently gifted men, some of whom, with truly superior genius, penetrated the profoundest depths of the Christian Faith, and placed in a brilliant light the secret and marvellous harmonies of the religion of Jesus Christ. When we read their profound and luminous writings, we may well feel proud and happy to be partakers of their belief. How resplendent with light and Divine beauty does

Catholic Doctrine appear in the works of these immortal theologians! How vast the powers of human reason! The chief mysteries in the natural and supernatural order of earth and heaven shine therein with mild, serene brightness. But we must not linger over this spectacle, consoling though it be amidst the sad attacks of men of our own day, who seem to fear that poor human reason must be lowered by seeking to draw light and heat from the clear, luminus focus of Faith. I must at once enter on the subject of St. Augustine's unbelief and ultimate return to the Faith.

CHAPTER IV.

St. Augustine—His unbelief and return to the Faith.

IS there any one who does not know that Augustine was a genius of the highest order, one of the most powerful intellects whom the world has ever produced ? Bossuet read and re-read him continually, ever finding fresh light in his writings. To his inspiration we owe the most eminent theologians and Christian philosophers of the middle ages and of modern times. We could point out writers who are more correct, more elegant, more eloquent, than the Bishop of Hippo ; but we believe that in the annals of mankind no intellect is to be met with superior to his. The experience of this man, as regards the question of unbelief and faith, is therefore worthy of particular attention.

By singular good fortune we possess a history of Augustine, written by himself, which gives us an intimate knowledge of his soul. His *Confessions* describe with great minuteness the twofold journey of this great soul, by which he descended into the darkness of infidelity and returned to the light of Faith. I know of no book more curious, more absorbing, more instructive, than this. I cannot attempt to reproduce the simple and dramatic picture of the wanderings and conversion of Augustine, but must content myself with pointing out some of its most characteristic features.

SECTION I.

How Augustine loses the Faith—He rapidly descends all the steps of unbelief—He falls into materialism and scepticism.

IN Augustine's time, society was in great part Christian, but still mingled with paganism. The Bishop of Hippo was born at Tagaste, in the year 384, of parents in the middle class. At the time of his birth his father was not a Christian, though he was converted afterward. But his mother, the future Saint Monica, had instructed him in the Faith of Jesus Christ from his tenderest years. "I then already believed," he says, " and my mother, and the whole household, except my father: yet did not he prevail over the power of my mother's piety in me, that as he did not yet believe, so neither should I."* However, the young Augustine had not received Baptism, he was only a Catechumen.

* *Conf.* lib. l. c. 11

The faith of the son of Monica was neither sufficiently earnest nor sufficiently enlightened to withstand the whirlwind of the passions; nor could it resist the poisonous action of a hostile or even indifferent school of teaching. Augustine's faith soon gave way; but still the name of Jesus Christ, which he had learned to venerate on his mother's knees, was always dear to his heart, even amidst his most grievous disorders.*

Augustine passed several years in the schools of Tagaste and Madaura, a neighboring city; then he was sent to the capital of Africa to finish his studies.

He tells us that his father, whose means were very moderate, was obliged to impose heavy sacrifices on himself, in order to enable his son to study under the famous masters of Carthage.† He was only sixteen when he arrived in that city. His soul was already a prey to sensual passions, and a residence in Carthage was not calculated to recall him to the austere performance of duty. He thought only of enjoyment; he knew no other pleasures than the gross and bitter pleasures of sense. "For within me was a famine of that inward food, thyself, my God; yet through that famine I was not hungered: but was without all longing for incorruptible sustenance, not because filled therewith, but the more empty, the more I loathed it. For this cause my soul was sickly and full of sores; it miserably cast

* *Conf.* lib. iii. c. 4.   † *Ibid.* lib. ii. c. 2.

itself forth, desiring to be relieved by the touch of objects of sense."* The students of Carthage were given up to all manner of disorders, and though Augustine was the slave of voluptuousness, he was better than many of his companions. According to the testimony of Vincent the Rogatist, he always loved decency and good manners even in his irregularities.† At the beginning of his residence at Carthage, the young student from Tagaste contracted a criminal intimacy with a woman which lasted fourteen years.

But the disorders of the son of Monica did not interfere with his progress in study; his quick intelligence triumphed over every obstacle. "Those studies," he says, "which were accounted commendable, had a view to excelling in the courts of litigation; the more bepraised, the craftier. Such is men's blindness, glorying even in their blindness. And now I was chief in the school of rhetoric, whereat I joyed proudly." ‡

The brilliant student of Tagaste soon became professor of rhetoric in the metropolis of Africa, and was no less successful as a master than he had been as a scholar.

But what had become of Augustine's religious belief in the midst of this whirlwind of pleasure and of the vain plaudits of the world? Where was the faith of his childhood? That faith was dead; Au-

---

* *Conf.* lib. iii. c. 1.   † Cf. *Conf.* lib. iii. c. 3.   ‡ *Ibid.*

gustine no longer believed the teaching of Christianity. His soul, it is true, preserved an affectionate respect for the name of Jesus Christ; but this respect, which was the fruit of his early education, found no support in his understanding, and subsisted only as a vague, unexplained sentiment. With virtue and innocence the son of Monica lost also his faith. Every Christian idea was effaced from his mind, and he entertained the most incredible prejudices against the Creed of the Church. He attributed the most extravagant doctrines to Christians. It was at this time he imagined that Christianity taught that God was a material being, with a body similar to ours! It is inexplicable how an intelligent man who had received a Christian education could seriously impute the grossest anthropomorphism to a religion which claims as one of its most glorious titles that it reëstablished in the human soul the grand idea of the spirituality and infinity of God. The religious teaching which Augustine received in his childhood must have been strangely superficial.

And with what had this poor, proud youth replaced the faith which had shone upon his cradle? He had, alas! descended to the lowest grade of intellectual misery. He had fallen into materialism, and into a doubly absurd form of materialism: into Manicheism. We know that the Manichees believed in two coeternal principles, wholly independent and essentially opposed to one another—the good principle and the evil principle. They professed the most shameful extravagances. It was at Carthage that Augustine fell in with these strange masters, who spoke much of truth and science, and set forth their pretensions to unveil all mysteries; and this noble genius, whose wings had been cut, as Plato speaks, by sensuality, allowed himself to be caught in their vulgar toils. "I fell among men," says he, "proudly doting, exceeding carnal, and prating, in whose mouths were the snares of the devil. . . . They cried out exceedingly, Truth, Truth, and spake much thereof to me, but the truth was not in them; but they spake falsehood, not of thee only, O my God! who truly art Truth, but even of those elements of this world, the work of thy hands."* . . . "Alas!" cries Augustine, after having recalled some of the errors of Manicheism, "by what steps was I brought down to the depths of hell? Ah my God! . . . I descended thither because I sought thee, not according to the understanding of the mind, wherein thou willedst that I should excel the beasts, but according to the sense of the flesh."†

It is needless to follow Augustine in the picture he draws of the errors and unheard-of absurdities into which Manicheism had led him.‡ It is sufficient to remark that he consulted astrologers, and believed all the follies of judicial astrology.§ Pascal says, "*None so credulous as unbelievers;*" and

* *Conf.* lib. iii. c. 10.   ‡ *Ibid.* lib. iii. c. 6.
† *Ibid.*   § *Ibid.* lib. iv. c. 3.

nothing is more true. The whole history of infidelity for eighteen hundred years confirms this assertion. People reject, in the name of reason, the Catholic Creed, reasonable though it be, and capable of solid demonstration, and they receive the most senseless superstitions without proof and against all reason. A very curious book might be written with this title, *The Credulity of Infidels;* and more than one interesting chapter might be furnished by the times in which we live.

Augustine had now become a thorough materialist. He admitted the existence of a God, but a God who was corporeal and extended; he could not conceive the existence of beings purely spiritual. He says: "When I wished to think on my God, I knew not what to think of but a mass of bodies, (for what was not such did not seem to me to be anything.) This was the greatest and almost only cause of my inevitable error. For hence I believed evil also to be some such kind of substance, and to have its own soul and hideous bulk. . . . And because a piety, such as it was, constrained me to believe that the good God never created any evil nature, I conceived two masses, contrary to one another, both unbounded; but the evil narrower, the good more expansive. And from this pestilent beginning, the other sacrilegious conceits followed."*
" I knew not God to be a spirit, and that conse-

---

* *Conf.* lib. v. c. 10.

quently he had neither a body composed of different members, nor one who hath parts extended in length and breadth, or whose being was bulk."*

Thus was this magnificent intellect stifled, as it were, in the folds of sensual passion: it could no longer conceive any reality in the world of intelligence; it could only recognize data apparent to the senses, and phantasms of the imagination which corresponded to them.

The spectacle of such a fall involuntarily recalls to me the pages of Plato, in which that profound observer points out that sensuality is the usual source of those shameful excesses into which the most highly gifted minds fall. "Take," says this true philosopher, "take these same souls from childhood, cut away and retrench all that the passion of lust deposits therein; free them from the heavy masses attached to the pleasures of the table and such like enjoyments; take away the weight which depresses the vision of the soul to inferior things, (περὶ τὰ χάτω.) Then if, freed from such obstacles, the same gaze, in the same men, is turned toward the things that are true, (εἰς τὰ ἀληθῆ,) it will behold them with the same penetration with which it now sees the objects to which it is turned."† Never did any man justify, in the same degree as Augustine, these words of the great disciple of Socrates.

---

* *Conf.* lib. iv. c. 3.   † *Republ.* lib. vii. 516.   Cf. lib. ix. 586.   *Tim.* 9ɔ.

Manicheism could not long satisfy this erring genius. He soon found therein weak points and important omissions, and his soul was beset with doubts. He was flattered with the hope that Faustus, the most famous teacher of the sect, would readily clear away his difficulties. But how was he deceived! He saw this incomparable doctor, and found him to be only a brilliant talker; he had no solution for those grave questions with which the anxious soul of Monica's son was tormented.* Augustine found himself cruelly deceived, and despaired of finding in Manicheism the light he was seeking; still he thought he ought not to break the ties which bound him to this gloomy sect. "As one finding nothing better," says he, "I had settled to be content meanwhile with what I had, in whatever way fallen upon, unless by chance something more eligible should dawn upon me." † In the year 383, the young professor left Carthage and repaired to Rome. He had grown weary of the turbulence and dissoluteness of the students of Carthage; he was told that the youth of the Roman schools were more docile and modest; moreover he flattered himself that he should attain fortune and glory more rapidly in the ancient capital of the world. ‡ He embarked without his mother's knowledge, who would have accompanied him, and whose heart was broken at the

---

* *Conf.* lib. v. c. 6, 7.   † *Ibid.* c. 7.   ‡ *Ibid.* lib. v. c. 8.

separation from her son.* He met with the Manichees again in Rome, and still joined himself with them. He was convinced the truth was not to be found with them, but he despaired of finding it elsewhere; and his weary spirit began to think that truth cannot be comprehended by man, and that possibly the Academics were the wisest of philosophers, for they doubt all things, and abstain from affirming anything.†

The brilliant dreams of the professor quickly vanished. "Students of rhetoric were not wanting to Augustine; the disorders which reigned at Carthage did not show themselves in the Roman schools, but in them turbulence was replaced by meanness. It often happened that the Roman scholars plotted together, and, to avoid paying their master's stipend, deserted his lessons in a body. Augustine felt profound contempt for such conduct; disgust soon followed contempt, and hearing that the city of Milan had requested Symmachus, prefect of Rome, to send thither a professor of rhetoric, he solicited and obtained the appointment. . . . Symmachus, prefect of Rome, was at the same time pontiff and augur, and was the same who shortly afterward begged of the emperors the restoration of the statue and altar of Victory. This defender of the old Roman divinities little thought that the young professor of

* *Conf.*   † *Ibid.* c. 10.

rhetoric, whose name was scarcely known to him, was destined to strike the last blow against the gods, to close the sepulchre of the old pagan world, and to plant over its immense tomb the Cross of Christ, the prophetic symbol of a glorious futurity."*

It was at Milan that Divine Providence awaited Augustine. There the pure light of truth was to open his weary, aching eyes, and restore to them that clear strong vision which they had lost through contact with passion and sophistry. God made use of an eloquent and holy Bishop to lead back this poor victim of error to the truth. We shall now see by what means.

SECTION II.

Augustine's return to the Faith—He passes through intellectual and moral crises before his conviction.

AUGUSTINE arrived at Milan toward the end of the year 384; he was just thirty years of age. The name of the Bishop of Milan was not unknown to him, for the fame of Ambrose filled the world.† The professor of rhetoric presented himself to the holy Bishop, who received him with the kindness of a father. "Thenceforth I began to love him,"

---

* M. Poujoulat, *Hist. de St. Augustin*, tom. i. c. 11. Cf. *Conf.* lib. v. c. 12, 13.
† " Notum orbi terræ."—*Conf.* lib. v. c. 13.

says Augustine; "at first indeed not as a teacher of the truth, (which I utterly despaired of in thy Church,) but as a person kind toward myself."* How marvellous, that a young man whose infancy had been cradled on the knees of a Christian mother should not even suspect that truth might be found in the Church of Jesus Christ! So strong were the prejudices with which the Manichees had inspired him against Christianity! If he went to hear Ambrose explain the doctrines of religion to his people, it was from pure literary curiosity and to enjoy the charms of his eloquence. "I listened diligently to him preaching to the people, not with that intent I ought, but, as it were, trying his eloquence, whether it answered to the fame thereof. . . . And I hung on his words attentively, but of the matter I was as a careless and scornful looker-on."† Are there not many in our days who listen to our great Christian orators with the like dispositions?

However, Augustine, though exclusively taken up with the outward form, could not long forbear acknowledging that the form in the sermons of Ambrose covered serious and solid foundation. By degrees his senseless prejudices against the Christian Religion gave way; finally he comprehended that Catholic belief was not so absurd as he had imagined, that it could be defended, and

* *Conf.*
† "Rerum autum incuriosus et contemptor astabam."—*Ibid.*

that the objections of the Manichees were not unanswerable.* But there he stopped. The Catholic Faith was not conquered, but neither did it appear to him to be victorious.† Is it credible that he could be still held back by the impossibility of conceiving a purely spiritual substance? However, his understanding definitely abandoned Manicheism; he judged that the tenets of most of the philosophers with regard to material objects were much more probable than the doctrine of the Manichees. Therefore he resolved to leave that sect. The school of the Academics, who doubt of everything alone appeared in harmony with the state of his mind. But as his early education had commended to him the Catholic Church, he resolved, amidst this universal doubt, to remain a Catechumen in the Church till something certain might dawn upon his soul."

Monica had crossed the sea and had joined her son at Milan. She rejoiced to learn that Augustine had renounced Manicheism. What tears and what prayers had this holy mother poured forth before God that the soul of her child might be enlightened, and that he might see clearly the monstrous and immoral errors of that sect! Now that God had heard her prayers on that point she wait-

* " Ipsa defendi posse mihi jam cœperunt videri ; et fidem Catholicam, pro qua nihil posse dici adversus oppugnantes Manichæos putaveram, jam non impudenter asseri existimabam."—*Conf.* c. 14.

† "Ita enim Catholica non mihi victa videbatur, ut nondum etiam victrix apparet."—*Ibid.*

ed patiently for him to complete his work. She was convinced that she should not die till she had seen her son restored to the Catholic Faith.

But this darkened intelligence had a long road to traverse before it could reach the full light of the Gospel. The idea of a Being, sovereignly perfect, shone in the inmost depth of his soul and seized hold of his conscience; but his understanding, accustomed to the gross imaginations of materialism, could not conceive any substance without material form.* Augustine was still the slave of his senses and imagination. At this time Divine Providence caused certain books of the Platonic philosophers to fall into his hands.† He read them eagerly, and their perusal worked the most salutary revolution in his mind. In them he saw that the sensible world, which he thought the only reality, is but the kingdom of shadows; that true realities are purely intellectual, and that God, who occupies the summit of the world of intelligence, is a pure spirit inaccessible to the senses and imagination. It was quite a revelation to this noble genius so long enslaved by matter. Quitting at length the world of phantoms to enter into that inward sanctuary where God shows himself, as Plato speaks, his soul found itself in finding God; it beheld itself by the aid of an intelligible light superior to

---

* *Conf.* lib. vii. c. 1.
† " Procurasti mihi per quemdam hominem . . . quosdam Platonicorum libros ex Græca lingua in Latinam versos."—*Ibid.* c. 9.

itself, a light unchangeable, identical with Truth.* Here was the end of materialism. The mind of Augustine, restored to itself, was replaced on the true path of Christian spiritualism.

It has been said that Plato's philosophy is the human preface to the Gospel.† Doubtless it is an incorrect and very imperfect preface, but it is a fact that Platonism was the vestibule of Christianity to Augustine as well as to other great intellects of the early centuries.

The books of the Platonists had revealed the invisible world to Augustine; but unhappily they had increased in him the pride of intellect without freeing him from the pride of the flesh, and this twofold pride is the principal obstacle to the light of Faith. The new disciple of Plato was proud of his wisdom; he did not feel that his necessities were infinite, he did not think of praying to God to supply them. Humility is the gate of Faith; prayer, which is the acknowledgment of a poverty which expects everything from God, is the most beautiful expression of humility. God wills that man, who is a mere creature, and moreover a fallen creature, should confess his own insufficiency and implore aid from on high.

This is the usual condition of the effusion of the supernatural light of Faith. Augustine was acquainted with the teaching of the Church on the

* *Conf.* c. 10 and 20.   † *Ibid.* c. 20.

Incarnation of the Word, and after he had read the Neo-Platonists he willingly believed in the Word; but the Incarnation, that mystery of the love and humiliation of God, offended his egotism and his pride. In his eyes, Jesus Christ was the wisest of men, but he was not the Word made Flesh.*

Augustine learnt two things from the study of St. Paul's Epistles which he had not found in the books of the Platonists : the lost state of man and the need of the grace of God to know and practise the truth. He comprehended the mystery of that twofold law, the law of the flesh and the law of the spirit, by the painful conflict by which his soul was torn. He possessed the key to those wonderful contradictions of which our nature is continually the theatre, and from which the Manichees drew an argument in favor of the absurd doctrine of two eternal principles—one good and the other evil, the respective causes of the good and evil which appear in us. Once convinced of the fall of man, and contemplating in himself the deadly traces of the fall, Augustine began to comprehend the benefit of the Incarnation; the sentiment of his moral and intellectual failings inspired him with humility ; the humiliation of the Word in the mystery of the Incarnation no longer appeared to him unworthy

* *Conf.* c. 19. Cf. c. 17.

of the majesty of God: Jesus Christ revealed himself to his soul as the true and necessary Restorer of fallen humanity.

Augustine relates that, whilst reading the Epistles of St. Paul, he experienced, by the secret operation of grace, sentiments of humility and compunction, leading him to shed tears and to confess his faults. He insists on this point, that humility is the source of true light, and repeats these words of Jesus Christ to his Father: "Thou hast hid these things from the wise and prudent, and hast revealed them to little ones."*

Formerly, when a student at Carthage, the son of Monica had desired to read the Holy Scriptures; but the simplicity of the Divine Books offended the pride of a young man accustomed to the majestic style of Cicero, and incapable of penetrating the mysterious depths of revealed doctrine: the study of these sublime pages was distasteful to him.† Since then, the Scriptures had not changed, but Augustine was no longer the same man; his understanding had ripened, his prejudices against Christianity had vanished; the sermons and example of Ambrose, the prayers and tears of Monica, had opened his eyes, and where he had formerly perceived only clouds and darkness, he now discovered an admirable light.

The moral and intellectual transformation of Au-

---

* *Conf.* c. 21.   † *Ibid.* lib. iii. c. 5.

gustine daily advanced. He was no longer tempted by the dreams of his youth, fortune and glory; but the flesh still held him captive, though the fire of passion was allayed. At this juncture, Augustine sought a venerable priest, Simplician, the spiritual father of Ambrose, to whom he opened his mind. Simplician related to him the conversion of Victorinus, a celebrated professor, whose Latin translations of the writings of the Platonic philosophers Augustine had read. The young African professor ardently desired to imitate this great man. His understanding was convinced of the truth of Christianity, but he was held back by his will. "I was bound," says he, "not with another's irons, but by my own iron will. My will the enemy held, and thence had made a chain for me, and bound me. For of a forward will was a lust made; and a lust served became custom; and custom not resisted became necessity. By which links, as it were, joined together (whence I called it a chain) a hard bondage held me enthralled. But that new will which had begun to be in me, freely to serve thee, and to wish to enjoy thee, O God! the only assured pleasantness, was not yet able to overcome my former wilfulness, strengthened by age. Thus did my two wills, one new and the other old—one carnal, the other spiritual—struggle within me; and by their discord undid my soul."*

---

* *Conf.* lib. viii. c. 5.

Augustine has depicted in the liveliest colors this grievous combat in which his salvation was at stake. The spiritual will, aided by the grace of God, can always vanquish the carnal will, and at last, after many failings, it completely triumphed in this tempest-tossed soul. "For to go toward thee, O my God!" cries Augustine, when relating this internal conflict, "and even to go in thither, was nothing else but to will to go, but to will resolutely and thoroughly; not to turn and toss, this way and that, a maimed and half-divided will, struggling, with one part sinking as another rose."*

Augustine has left us the picture of the last crisis through which his soul passed before breaking its chains. It is a marvellously touching scene. He was in the garden of the house he occupied at Milan, and was alone with his friend Alypus, from whom he had no secrets. A mighty storm agitated his mind, and he felt the need of tears. Alypus perceived it, and abstained from following his friend, when he rose to leave him. Augustine cast himself on the ground under a fig-tree, and there shed torrents of tears, intermingled with prayers and pious groans. All at once a voice issued from a neighboring house, like the voice of a young boy or girl chanting, and often repeating these words: "Take up and read; take up and read." "Instantly my countenance altered," says Augustine. "I

---

* *Conf*. c. 8.

began to think most intently whether children were wont in any kind of play to sing such words; nor could I remember ever to hear the like. So, checking the torrent of my tears, I arose, interpreting it to be no other than a command of God to open the Book and read the first chapter I should find. For I had heard of Antony, that coming in during the reading of the Gospel, he received the admonition, as if what was being read was spoken to him: 'Go sell what thou hast and give to the poor, and thou shalt have treasure in Heaven: and come follow me.'* Eagerly then I returned to the place where Alypus was sitting, for there had laid the volume of the Apostle when I arose thence. I seized opened, and in silence read that section on which my eyes first fell: 'Let us walk, not in rioting and drunkenness, not in chambering and impurities, not in contention and envy, but put ye on the Lord Jesus Christ, and make not provision for the flesh in its concupiscences.'† No further would I read, nor needed I; for instantly at the end of this sentence, by a light, as it were, of serenity infused into my heart, all the darkness of doubt vanished away.

"Then putting my finger between, or some other mark, I shut the volume, and with a calm countenance made it known to Alypus. And what was wrought in him which I knew not, he thus showed me. He asked to see what I had read. I showed

---

* Matt. xix. 21.   † Rom. xiii. 13, 14.

him, and he looked even further than I had read, and I knew not what followed. This followed, 'Him that is weak in the faith take unto you;'* which he applied to himself and disclosed to me. And by this admonition was he strengthened; and by a good resolution and purpose, and most corresponding to his character, wherein he did always very far differ from me, for the better, without any turbulent delay he joined me. Thence we go in to my mother; we tell her; she rejoiceth; we relate in order how it took place; she leaps for joy, and triumpheth." †

Well might this holy mother triumph and leap for joy! Her tears and supplications were heard, all her desire was accomplished. Vigorous souls do nothing by halves. From the moment that Augustine, yielding to the attraction of grace, had said, "I believe," he gave himself wholly to the truth; the most austere practices of the Christian religion alone appeared to satisfy the ardor of his generous will. This man, who but yesterday could not comprehend the possibility of living if deprived of gross carnal pleasures, now determined to sacrifice even the lawful joys of marriage, and to live in perpetual chastity. It is well known how faithfully he kept his resolution.

The conversion of Augustine happened in the month of August of the year 386, when he was

---

* Rom. xiv. 1. † *Conf.* lib. viii. c. 12.

thirty-two years old. He was baptized by St. Ambrose on Easter Eve in 387. Four years later he was ordained Priest at Hippo, and toward the end of the year 395 he received episcopal consecration.

It would be rash to say what the genius of Augustine might have become had it not bent before the authority of the Church; none, I think, can take it upon themselves to maintain that the Christian Faith was an obstacle to the development of this powerful intellect. It is true, it is incontestable that Faith was at once a marvellous light and a wonderful moral power to this great mind. Faith opened to him horizons absolutely new, suffered him freely to use his wings and to traverse with incomparable ease and security those regions in which human reason is naturally called to exercise itself. I will venture to remind the reader of a passage I have elsewhere written on this subject: " Would you understand, would you see with your own eyes how far Faith restores, enlarges, elevates reason? Open the works of Plato and of St. Augustine. Whilst you glance over the writings of these two immortal minds you will be struck by the eminent doctrinal superiority of the Christian Bishop over the Prince of Grecian Philosophers. First, all the truths which are in Plato are to be found in St. Augustine, but with a purity, a clearness, a firmness, a plenitude, which we vainly seek in the Athenian philosopher. Plato's view is frequently obscured even on the ground of natural religion, in matters which are within the province of reason; he sees but a part of the truth, he mixes error with it, and almost always is deficient in firmness even on those points which he seems best to understand. And yet every one is agreed that mere human reason never had a more intelligent, more luminous, more complete interpreter than the disciple of Socrates. Plato is indisputably the noblest and most exalted representative of reason devoid of the light of Faith. But reason, how high soever it may soar, is full of obscurity and subject to a thousand weaknesses, even in that part of the moral and religious domain which naturally falls to it. Reason has lost its uprightness, and needs the renovating grace of Faith in order to regain it and exercise its full power. To Faith the Bishop of Hippo owes his incomparable superiority to the master of the Academy on all great questions of the rational and strictly philosophical order." *

* *Les Dogmes Catholiques*, etc., vol. iii. pp. 302, 303. Paris, 1860.

CHAPTER V.

The Christian Faith of the Middle Ages—It is paramount in society, and governs men of high intellect as well as the common people—Was this a blind Faith?

AT the period of tne great Bishop of Hippo's death, the Roman Empire was crumbling away on all sides under the repeated inroads of the barbarians. This old-world empire was condemned to perish; for in spite of the work of moral renovation which it had undergone, it still retained a fund of ideas and customs which unfitted it for the office of forming Christian society. The Church required other elements to found a new civilization. Moreover, it was needful that the justice of God should be exercised upon an empire which had trodden under foot all laws of the moral order, and which for three centuries had shed the blood of the disciples of the Incarnate Word.

This is not the place to remind the reader how Christianity gained possession of those vigorous and healthful races, uncultivated and savage though they were, which established themselves on the ruins of the Roman Empire. A new social order arose from the bleeding ruins with which the invasion of the barbarians had strewn the soil of Europe. By dint of patience and holy energy, the Church had contrived to bind together by close ties nations proud of their savage independence, and whilst she respected individual nationality, she founded that social unity which is expressed by the beautiful name of Christendom. The European nations of the Middle Ages were all united by a common Faith; they all recognized the same authority; they all obeyed the Church as their common mother.

Every one admits that the Christian Faith was supreme during the Middle Ages. People even allow pretty generally that Faith was a useful auxiliary to social and moral progress. "The Church," says one of the most ardent adversaries of Catholicism, " occupies one step in the immense ladder of the development of humanity. Her existence is intimately united with the destinies of those barbarous nations who destroyed the Roman Empire; she was called upon to raise them by faith to a state of morality and intelligence. The Church was worthy of her mission, for in an age of barbarism, immorality, and ignorance she alone opened asylums for science, she alone showed to the world models of Christian perfection; she wielded spiritual power in the highest acceptation of the word, for she ruled by superiority of reason and wisdom. But this rule, by its very nature, was transitory. The world is no longer the world of the Middle Ages; it is no longer a prey to brute force; it no longer requires a power to educate, rule, and guide it like a child, by blind faith."* People recognize, therefore, in a certain degree, the benefits of Catholic Faith in the Middle Ages, but they pretend that the nations of that period were nations of children, and that the Faith which served for their intellectual and moral education was a blind Faith.

I am not going to discuss this twofold thesis, but I must say a few words in elucidation of the grave question whether infidelity is really the natural and legitimate result of the progress of reason.

The Middle Ages comprise two essentially distinct periods. In the first period we see the nations who replaced the old Roman society still barbarians; they are without moral and intellectual culture; they have the impetuosity, the heat, the inconstancy, the simplicity of childhood. In the second period we behold these same nations, but entirely changed; they have grown up; they have completed their education; they are truly civilized. The French of St. Louis differ as widely from the Franks of Clovis as a grown-up man differs from a child. Now it is an incontestable fact that the

---

* *Studies on the History of Humanity: the Papacy and the Empire.* By F. Laurent, Professor at the University of Ghent. p. 54.

Christian Faith ruled over both these periods of the Middle Ages.

I frankly avow that I cannot repress a smile of pity when I hear certain persons speak disdainfully of the darkness of that grand historic epoch, and date the advent of light to the world from the sixteenth century. If so, who raised those cathedrals, those public edifices, those palaces of learning and piety, those monuments of genius faith, patriotism—wonders of architecture—which still in our days constitute the noblest monuments of the soil of Europe? Were these marvels of art bequeathed to us by nations of children? Do not *they* rather deserve the name of children who, in the face of these living witnesses to the genius and energetic activity of their fathers, insult and outrage a glorious past? Blind, ungrateful children, who blush not to curse the hand to whose skill and bounty they owe a good part of the patrimony they enjoy.

I am not a fanatical admirer of the Middle Ages; I believe there were many imperfections, many disorders, many abuses in those powerful bodies which were bound together by a common Faith, a common submission to the authority of the Church. But men must indeed be blind if they fail to recognize that this period had points of incomparable greatness.

If, as people affirm, the Faith of the Catholic populations of the Middle Ages was an unenlightened Faith, they must at least admit that it was not the fault of the Church, for in all parts of Europe she opened sources of instruction: schools arose everywhere by the side of cathedrals, colleges, and convents, and some of these acquired great celebrity. Great Britain, Italy, Spain, France, Belgium, Germany, Bohemia, Denmark, all Catholic countries, had universities, or upper and universal schools, in which all the sciences were taught.* Centres of light were not wanting in Europe: therefore why not admit that learned men of the highest order were nourished in her bosom?

I willingly admit that in the Middle Ages historical criticism, mathematics, natural sciences, were not cultivated with that ardor and success which in modern times have acquired for them immortal glory. But I believe that the science of Religion, the science of the dogmas taught by the Church, was never treated with more vigor, penetration, and power at any period of the history of Christianity, than in the age of St. Anselm, of Hugh and Richard, of St. Victor, of St. Bonaventure, St. Thomas Aquinas, and Duns Scotus. No period has surpassed the Middle Ages in the philosophy of Christianity, or in the accurate and profound study of the principles and the dogmas

---

* See Hunter. *Tableau des Institutions et des Mœurs de l'Eglise au Moyen Age*, tom. iii. chap. xxxv.

of Catholic Faith. What was the motto of those men whom ignorant or prejudiced detractors depict as blindly believing all the teaching of the Church? We read it in the title which St. Anselm had at first intended to give to his *Proslogium*, an admirable little treatise on metaphysics: "Fides quærens intellectum." This is the device of all the masters of scholastic theology. They have faith, they firmly believe all the Church teaches; but they are not content with believing; they desire as much as possible to understand; they seek to give an account of their faith, to analyze and penetrate its dogmas, and thus to attain that science of faith which constitutes true Catholic Theology. "Credo ut intelligam,"* says St. Anselm. I seek not to understand the mysteries of Christianity before I adhere to them by faith. I accept them on the authority of the Divine Revelation made known by the Church; but when this faith is once established, I endeavor to penetrate its mysteries. My belief helps me on the way to science. I believe in order that I may understand. "As it is necessary that we believe the mysteries of the Christian Faith before we discuss them by reason, so does it also appear to me negligence not to seek to understand that which we firmly believe."†

* *Proslog.* c. i.
† "Sicut rectus ordo exigit, ut profunda Christiane fidei credamus priusquam ea præsumamus ratione discutere: ita negligentia mihi videtur, si postquam confirmati sumus in fide, non studemus quod credimus intelligere."—*Cur. Deus Homo*, lib. i. c. 2.

Most of the writings of the great Archbishop of Canterbury are an eloquent carrying out of this thought: whilst he rests firmly on faith he aims at raising himself to the understanding of Christian truths. At the commencement of the work from which we have just quoted, the disciple of Anselm asks to be led "to understand by reason that all which the Catholic Faith commands to be believed of Christ ought really to be believed."* The master accedes to his disciple's request, and seeks to explain how the Incarnation of the Son of God was necessary for the accomplishment of the designs of Providence for the Salvation of man. He seeks not to conceal the difficulties which infidelity opposes to the mystery of the Incarnation; he points out and discusses all these difficulties on the ground of reason. Men who speak with so much disdain of the *blind faith* of the Middle Ages, would do well to read this short treatise on the Incarnation.

The spirit of St. Anselm was that of all the eminent scholastics. A celebrated theologian of the twelfth century, Richard of St. Victor, has left us a singularly remarkable work on the Trinity. At the beginning of the book, Richard declares Faith to be the starting-point and necessary foundation of all theological science. "Faith," he says, "is the entrance-gate of the sanctuary; by Faith alone

---

* *Cur Deus Homo*, præf.

can we penetrate therein. But," he adds directly afterward, "we must not pause on the threshold of the sanctuary, we must penetrate into the interior, we must use every means in order that each day we may daily advance further in the knowledge of the truths received by Faith."* "If the beginning of all good," says this illustrious doctor in another place, " resides in Faith, the consummation and completion of all good is found in science. Let us labor to attain this perfection, let all serve as steps by which we may go from Faith to science; let us use every effort to understand what we believe. It is of small account to have true and just sentiments with regard to God; we must, as I have just said, endeavor to understand what we believe; we must labor unceasingly, as much as we are permitted, as much as is possible, that we may grasp by reason what we hold by faith." †

Nor was Richard satisfied to establish principles with regard to the mission of theology; he preached also by example. His work on the Trinity contains a truly profound discussion of this great mystery; and though there are weak points in his book, it seems to me a sublime masterpiece of metaphysical science.‡

The generality of assailants of the Catholic

---

* *De Trinitate*, lib. i. c. 3.   † *Ibid.* prolog.
‡ See *Coup d'Œil sur l'Histoire de la Théologie Dogmatique*, pp. 63–66. Laforet.

Faith seem to imagine that before modern times the grounds and teaching of that Faith had never been verified by the light of reason—had never formed the subject of scientific discussion. We have already had abundant evidence of the value of such an opinion. Moreover, the Middle Ages have bequeathed to us the writings of one who is illustrious above all doctors of the Church, and whose writings would suffice, even in these days, victoriously to refute all the objections of infidel philosophy to the Catholic Creed. This profound and universal genius has founded, with a power which has never been surpassed, the whole basis of Christianity; he has explained and justified its dogmas, its practices; he has proposed and solved all the difficulties which can offer themselves to the human intelligence. His works are the most marvellous expression of the alliance between reason and Faith. This man, whom it is scarcely necessary to name, is St. Thomas Aquinas.

It is impossible to enter with any degree of minuteness into the labors of this great doctor; but I consider it incumbent on me to show the point of view which he occupies in one of his great monumental works.

St. Thomas has written a work which we should now call a demonstration of the Catholic Religion; it is his *Summa against the Gentiles.* He explains the design of the work as follows : " Full of confidence in the Divine Mercy, I take upon myself to fill the office of a sage; and though the undertaking is beyond my strength, I intend, according to my feeble means, to demonstrate the truth professed by the Catholic Faith, and to repel all errors contrary to it. For, to make use of the words of Hilary, I feel that the first duty which I have to fulfil toward God, during my life, is to consecrate my writings and all the faculties of my soul to the task of making him known. But it is difficult, for two reasons, to attack each error in particular. The first reason is, that we are not sufficiently acquainted with the sacrilegious inventions of erring minds, to draw from their very teaching arguments capable of overthrowing their errors. This method was pursued by the ancient fathers, to destroy the erroneous doctrines of the Gentiles, whose dogmas they knew because they themselves had been of the number of the Gentiles, or at all events had lived amongst them and studied their doctrines. The second reason is, that amongst them there are some, such as the Mohammedans and pagans, who do not agree with us in recognizing the authority of Scripture, which might convince them. We can dispute with the Jews, taking the Old Testament in support of our arguments, in the same way as we make use of the New Testament in opposing heretics. But pagans and Mohammedans admit neither the one nor the other. Therefore, it is necessary to have recourse to natural reason, to which all are obliged to submit, although reason alone suffices not in

Divine matters. At the same time that I examine each truth, I shall point out the errors which it excludes, and I shall show how truth which is susceptible of demonstration accords with the Christian Faith."*

It is therefore a complete apology of the Christian Faith which St. Thomas undertakes to write, taking his stand on the ground of reason. He distinguishes two orders of truths in the Catholic Creed, some rational, others super-rational. "In those things which we confess in regard to God," says he, "there is a twofold mode of truth. In fact there are truths which exceed the power of human reason: as, that God is three and one. There are others to which human reason can attain: as, for example, that God is, that God is one, and other similar truths, which the philosophers themselves have proved to demonstration with regard to God, guided by the light of natural reason."† The great apologist explains why it was fitting that rational truths themselves should be proposed to man as the object of Divine Faith;‡ he points out the causes for the revelation of truths superior to reason,§ and proves that Christians do not lightly believe these super-rational truths. He fixes, in the following terms, the principles which govern the question of the agreement between reason and faith. "Although the truth of the Christian Faith surpasses the capa-

---

* *Contra Gent.* lib. i. c. 2.   † *Ibid.* c. 3.   ‡ *Ibid.* c. 4. § *Ibid.* c. 5.

city of human reason, it is impossible that it should be in opposition to the data which form the basis of reason. In fact, first, it is evident that the natural data of reason are most true, so much so that it is not possible to think that they may be false. It is not permitted to look upon that which appertains to faith as false, because it is too manifestly confirmed by God. As that which is false is opposed to that which is true, . . . it is impossible that the truth of the Christian Faith can be in opposition to the principles which are naturally known by reason. Secondly, . . . The principles which we know naturally are placed in us by a Divine hand, for God himself is the author of our nature. Therefore these principles are also in the Divine Wisdom; and consequently all that is contrary to them is opposed to the wisdom of God, and cannot for that reason, come from God. We must therefore conclude that the articles of Faith, which have been divinely revealed, cannot be contrary to natural knowledge. . . . It follows evidently, from what goes before, that whatever objections may be made against the teaching of faith, they cannot be taken legitimately from first natural principles known by themselves. Consequently they can have no demonstrative force; they are only plausible reasons or sophisms, which it is easy to refute.* "As faith," says the angelic doctor in another place, "rests on infallible truth, and as it is impossible to

---

* *Contra Gent.* c. 7.

demonstrate the contrary of truth, it is evident that the proofs alleged against faith are not demonstrations, but arguments that may be solved."*

The *Summa against the Gentiles* comprises four books. The first three are devoted to questions of the rational order; the last treats of superrational truths. In the first book, the author considers, by the method of reason, that which concerns God in himself; in the second, he discusses the manner in which creatures proceed from him ; in the third, he examines the relation of creatures toward him, as toward their end. In, the fourth book, St. Thomas sets forth and discusses the Catholic Doctrine of the Trinity, the Sacraments, the Resurrection of the Body, the State of the Soul after Death, and the Last Judgment. The whole Christian edifice, from the foundation to the summit, is examined in this magnificent work, and that with a power of reasoning before which modern criticism, provided it be sincere, must reverently bow. Never has the Christian Faith been subjected, in its principles and in its dogmas, to a more complete and serious scrutiny.†

If those who speak with so much disdain of the Faith of the Middle Ages would read the *Summa against the Gentiles*, the *Theological Summa*, (another incomparable monument of St. Thomas,) the *Opus-*

---

* Plato had already said that that which is true cannot be refuted.
† *Summa Theol.* part i. q. 1. a. 8.

cula, and his *Biblical Commentaries*, they would be forced to admit that the Faith which they call blind and unreasoning is marvellously enlightened, and that in the hands of genius it becomes a power which sustains, purifies, enlarges reason, and raises it to a sublime grandeur unknown to mere human philosophy.

The whole of European society in the Middle Ages, with the exception of the Mohammedans, whose religious creed is beneath discussion, was Christian, and earnest in the profession of the Faith. Still we may discover in its bosom a certain number of unbelievers. Scotus Erigena, Amaury of Chartres, and David of Dinan must be regarded as such, and they all three professed pantheism.* The first has left us two considerable works, but we possess no writings of the others. The serious error into which these writers fell does not testify to the rectitude of their minds.† No one can dream of comparing them, for power of reasoning, with the men I have just named, or with the many other illustrious philosophers and theologians who were the glory of the Church of the Middle Ages. Alcuin, Lanfranc, St. Anselm, Hildebert of Mans, Hugh and Richard of St. Victor, Peter Lombard, Alexander of Halés, Albertus Magnus, Vincent of Beauvais,

---

* Abelard was a rationalist for some time, but did not remain one.

† See the excellent work of our lamented friend, Nicholas Möller: *Johannes Scotus Erigena und seine Irrthümer*. Mayence, 1844.

Roger Bacon, St. Thomas, St. Bonaventure, Henry of Ghent, Duns Scotus, Dante, Gerson, Nicholas of Cusa, were all sincere believers. Who will dare to maintain that they were not at the same time the honor of theology, philosophy, science, and literature?

We may, therefore, be allowed to conclude that if in the Middle Ages men believed with a firm and constant faith all the teaching of the Christian Religion, they did not believe blindly.

Now we must examine whether it was really the progress of science which brought about the great religious schism of modern times which is called Protestantism, and which led to infidelity, its natural consequence.

CHAPTER VI.

Protestantism and Reason.*

I AM often tempted to think that I must be under the influence of a bad dream, or that I must be the victim of some hallucination, when, on one side, I daily hear the Catholic Faith and the Church anathematized in the name of reason, human dignity, and civilization; and on the other, Protestantism and infidelity, the offspring of Protestantism, lauded to the skies. I ask myself—Can these outcries be sincere? Can reasonable beings be really met with in Europe capable of pronouncing and repeating with apparent conviction such an opinion? But I call to mind that in the infancy of Christianity the pious and chaste ministers of Nero, Domitian, Caligula, and similar monsters were seen hurrying to death, as guilty of impiety and immorality, those who were the sole representatives of

---

* God forbid that in the following pages I should dream of wounding, or even paining, our separated brethren ! But it is necessary to recall the fact that the unhappy men who, in the sixteenth century, caused this fatal and irremediable schism in Christian society were enemies alike to reason and to social virtue. Protestants of the present day are victims of this deplorable revolution. We pity them ; we judge them not. We would not insult the misery of a son whose parents had squandered his inheritance.

truth, virtue, and moral and religious dignity. I remember the numberless proofs of the levity, folly, moral and intellectual perversion of humanity in all ages; and I comprehend that in these days men may still be found who imagine that they are serving the cause of reason, justice, and social progress when they devote to public execration that grand institution and those sublime doctrines which form the safeguards of what they hold so dear. Doubtless this is a sad and frightful phenomenon; but it is perfectly understood by those who consider what human nature is, and have not forgotten its history.

The most determined enemies of the Catholic Faith are willing to admit that the Church was a precious auxiliary to civilization in the Middle Ages, in the midst of those half-barbarous, turbulent, unsettled races from whose bosom issued the well-ordered glories of the modern world; but they pretend that since the advent of Protestantism, the Church has but curtailed the legitimate development of reason, and that the Catholic Faith has been but a perpetual obstacle to the advancement of science and social progress. Luther's revolt against the authority of the Pope is hailed as the signal for the deliverance of the human intellect, and men admire the authors of the Reformation of the sixteenth century as the emancipators of reason and the restorers of the dignity of man. Not, however, they willingly confess, that human reason was set entirely free by the Protestant revolution. To Rationalism appertains the glory of giving full, entire freedom to this noble captive; but Protestantism was the first glorious stage on the route of definitive emancipation; and since, by the natural and necessary progress of events, Protestantism must bring forth Rationalism, it has a right to claim the honors of having broken the chains of humanity and saved reason by restoring its power. This is the thesis which an infidel press is daily defending, and many persons even elevate this thesis to the height of a philosophical and historical axiom above the reach of discussion.

We have a profound respect for axioms, but on condition that they really are axioms and do not contradict all principles and facts. We will ask leave, then, freely to examine and discuss this strange axiom, which our understanding has an invincible repugnance to accept.

We will begin by declaring that, with the adversaries of the Catholic Faith, we recognize the close affinity between Protestantism and Rationalism, and that we consider the latter to be not only the natural, but the legitimate offspring of the former. In our eyes Rationalism is, *de jure* as well as *de facto*, the child of Protestantism. But this is the limit of our agreement. Far from reason having obtained restitution of its legitimate dominion and its rights from Protestantism and Rationalism, we believe that they have seriously injured reason, and that it would have been irretrievably ruined if the Catholic Church, which is the vigilant and incorruptible guardian of all rights and all principles, had not unceasingly opposed their pernicious action. Many persons, we know, will look upon this opinion as a supreme paradox, but there are certain paradoxes which can be more easily justified than certain axioms. Let us cast a rapid glance over the page of history, and let history decide in which of these two contradictory theses truth is to be found.

It will suffice to take the most salient points of the moral and intellectual history of modern times, and to abide by the evidence of patent and undisputed facts.

SECTION I.

Primitive Protestantism—Age of Leo X.—The real Doctrine of Luther and his Accomplices—Denial of Reason and Liberty—War declared against Science—Immediate Effects of these Doctrines.

THE age which gave birth to Protestantism bears the name of a Pope; it is the age of Leo X. It appears to me that this simple fact ought to suffice to shake the thesis of the calumniators of the Church. At the moment when Luther raised the standard of revolt, the Pontifical court was the principal centre of the scientific, literary, and artistic movement in Europe; it was the rendezvous of artists, authors, philosophers; of men who excelled in every branch of intellectual culture. Leo X., the generous protector of genius, sought to assemble round him the *élite*, not only of Italy, but of Europe. What sovereign ever had a more brilliant circle of scholars; above all, of artists? Would not Leonardo da Vinci, Raphael, Michael Angelo, suffice to render any age illustrious? And it was in this age, so rich in intellectual greatness, and presided over by a Pope, that Protestantism appeared, as our adversaries say, to set free and reinstate human intellect. Does it not seem as if pleasantry were carried too far; and would it not be the time to repeat Horace's saying, "*Risum teneatis*"? But let us now see in what sense Luther and his accomplices understood the emancipation of reason and the re-establishment of human dignity.

Protestantism, at its birth, appeared not only as a revolt against the religious authority of the Pope, but at the same time as a protest against the principles and moral teaching of Christianity, even against that part of Christian Doctrine which appertains to natural religion; in a word, against reason purified and restored to all its rights by

Christianity. There are two very distinct points in the Reformation of the sixteenth century : a negative principle, and positive doctrines. The negative principle springs from the very fact of the revolt against the authority of the Church; it consists in the rejection of all external authority in matters of religion. But what did Luther teach when he had denied the authority of the Pope, and established the principle of the independence of each individual Christian ? What are his positive doctrines ? Considered in relation to reason and the foundations of moral order, what symbol did he substitute for the Catholic " Credo "? Here is the teaching of this singular liberator of the human mind : By original sin man has lost all strength, all power to know truth and to do good; his moral and religious faculties are not only weakened, but destroyed; he has become essentially wicked; reason, in so far as it relates to God and to that which concerns the moral order, no longer exists; liberty is but a word.*

Luther wrote a book, expressly against freewill, and he has ventured to give to his book this title, (*De Servo Arbitrio,*) *The Slave Will.* He pretends that philosophy introduced the word liberty as well as the fatal term reason, among Christians. He sets himself with savage violence against philosophy and against all the works of

---

* See Möhler, *Symbolik*, lib. i. ch. ii. § vi.

human reason. He frequently denounces such works as the works of Satan. Listen for a moment to this extraordinary emancipation of the human intellect: "If the Christian Revelation evidently rejects flesh and blood, that is, human reason and all that comes from man, . . . it follows, without doubt, that all this can be only darkness and lies. Yet the great schools, these schools of the devil, do not make the less noise about their natural lights, and cry them up to us as if they were not only useful, but even indispensable, to the manifestation of Christian truth; so that we may now be perfectly satisfied that these schools are an invention of the devil, destined to obscure Christianity, if not to ruin it utterly, as in fact they are on the high-road to do."* This is the way in which Luther speaks of those great schools, those universities which the Catholic Church had established in all parts of Europe, and which diffused everywhere the benefits of science. The reformer's hatred of universities amounted to madness. Among other follies, he pretended that the four soldiers who are said to have crucified our Lord, were the symbolical figure of the universities with their four faculties.† In his explanation of St. Paul's Epistle to the Galatians, he teaches that

---

* *Kircher postill. Walch*, xi. 459, ap. Döllinger. "La reforme, son développement intérieur et les résultats qu'elle a produits dans le sein de la société luthérienne."—Tom. i. p. 450, de la trad. fran. Paris, 1848.

† Döllinger, *ibid.*

faith ought to trample reason under foot, or, as he expresses it, strangle the beast. In the last sermon which he preached at Wittemberg, he says, amongst other things impossible to translate, "Reason is the bride of the devil, a prostitute, an abomination, which with its wisdom we ought to tread under foot."

Luther's writings are full of similar amenities with regard to reason.

I willingly admit that Calvin, Zuingle, and other leaders of the Reformation, did not wage so ferocious a war against human reason. But all the chiefs of Protestantism are agreed on these two points: Man is not free; good works are useless to salvation. Now, I ask, do not these two articles of the new creed entail, together with the denial of reason and the dignity of man, the destruction of all moral order, of all progress, of all civilization? To set up fatalism as a dogma, to proclaim the uselessness of good works—what is this but to destroy the very idea of duty, to destroy all morality, to reduce man to the level of brutes? Had these monstrous dogmas been generally received by the nations of Europe, so as to influence their daily life, and had they become the rule and motive of their actions, there would have been an end of civilization, and we should now be plunged in that abject and decrepit barbarism in which Mussulman nations, which profess fatalism and know no more powerful or salutary idea of duty, are vainly struggling. Happily for Europe, "public opinion, good sense, decency," as Balmez well remarks, " ranged themselves on the side of Catholicity. Even those nations which embraced these fatal doctrines as a religious theory, ordinarily rejected them in practice. Catholic teaching had left too deep an impression on these important points; too powerful an instinct of civilization had been communicated to European society by Catholic Doctrine. Thus did the Church, whilst she rejected the fatal errors taught by Protestantism, preserve society from the debasement which fatalist doctrines carry in their train. By condemning these errors of Luther, which formed, as it were, the main point of Protestantism at its birth, the Pope," adds the eminent Spanish politician, raised the war-cry against an irruption of barbarism in the order of ideas; he favored morality, law, public order, society, the Vatican. By securing the noble sentiment of liberty in the sanctuary of the conscience, he preserved the dignity of man; by combating Protestant ideas. By defending the sacred deposit confided to its keeping by the Divine Master, the Roman See became the tutelar divinity of the future destiny of civilization." *

The vigorous spiritual temperament which Eu-

* *Le Protestantisme comparé au Catholicisme dans ses rapports avec la Civilisation Européenne*, tom. i. ch. xi.

rope had received from the action of the Church for so many centuries past, enabled it to resist the abject and criminal follies of the father of the Reformation, but not without receiving serious and irreparable injury. It is enough to hear Luther himself despairingly attest the disastrous effects of these senseless doctrines; it is enough to hear this pretended restorer of the dignity of man deplore the frightful spiritual degradation which immediately followed the establishment of Protestantism. " Since the tyranny of the Pope has ceased among us," says the great Reformer, " there is no one who does not despise pure and salutary doctrine: it is no longer with men that we have to do, but with very brutes, with a brutish race."* . . . " People think only of deceiving one another; they take delight only in robbery and rapine: it appears as if the Word of Life had the property of changing men all at once into so many savage and furious beasts."† " Under the Papacy people performed with zeal, pleasure, and often at great expense, a number of those useless and senseless works. . . . Since they have heard the word liberty, they speak of nothing else, and use it only to refuse to fulfil every kind of duty. If I am free, say they, I may do what appears to me good. If I cannot be saved by works, why should I impose privations on myself, as, for example, by bestowing

---

* *Explic. du 1er liv. de Moise.* Valch. i. 615, ap. Döllinger.
† Ap. Döllinger, *Die Reformation*, etc., tom. i. p. 343.

alms on the poor? Their conduct is sevenfold worse under the reign of liberty than it formerly was under Papal tyranny.* . . . Theft and robbery are the only things about which people show any zeal.† . . . Whilst half the town of Wittemburg is threatened with ruin on account of adultery, usury, dishonesty, and rapine, there is not even a tribunal of justice to rectify all this misery.‡ . . . Formerly, when people were yet in the errors of Popery, if any good work were in question, all were ready and full of good will; now, on the contrary, they think only of heaping up riches, of saving, of robbing, of stealing the property of others by lies, deception, usury. If we still possess some evangelical pulpits and some Christian schools, it is not because people have paid the necessary expenses from their own stores: they found what they wanted by pillaging ancient foundations, which is not very meritorious. . . . Had the existence of churches and schools depended on our generosity, on us who live in this age, there would have been long ago neither scholars nor pastors."§ "We have a singular spectacle before our eyes; everyone pretends to be a Christian and follower of the Gospel, and yet they give themselves without measure to gluttony, avarice, usury, and I know not what other vices."‖

Here we have the confession of the father of

* Ap. Döllinger, *Die Reformation*, etc., tom. i. pp. 296, 297.
† *Ib.* p. 298. ‡ *Ib.* p. 304. § *Ib.* pp. 303, 304 ‖ *Ib.* p. 306.

Protestantism to show us how far this magnificent Reform had elevated and ennobled souls. True, Luther is filled with indignation when it is pointed out to him that this moral and intellectual decline is the natural and necessary fruit of his preaching and teaching. This indignation, if sincere, is certainly singular. When people have been taught that reason is of no account in the moral and religious order, that liberty is but a word, moreover, that good works are useless, can it be wondered at if they abstain from such works as impose constraint on their appetites and selfishness; if they indulge all their inordinate inclinations, despise intellectual culture, and descend even below the level of brutes?

We have seen that Luther was not satisfied with accusing reason of absolute want of power in the moral and religious order; but that he deemed it to be evil, to be contrary to faith, and that he attacked all culture of the reason, and especially philosophy, with the grossest sarcasms. These senseless declamations had their effect. Schools and academies were suppressed in many places where the new religion was established. "At Wittemburg," says Döllinger, "the preachers George Mohr and Gabriel Didymus, both zealous Lutherans, proclaimed from the pulpit that the study of the sciences was not only useless but pernicious, and that people could not do better than destroy academies and schools. The result of this preaching was to convert the school-house of Wittemburg into a baker's shop. The same thing occurred throughout the duchy of Anspach."* Protestant magistrates, alarmed at the desertion and ruin of the schools, addressed a petition to the Margrave of Brandenburg, in which they declared, "If this state of things continue we shall soon fall into such gross ignorance that nothing will be more difficult than to find a good preacher or a skilful lawyer."†

Catholicism had covered Germany with schools and academies, besides a vast number of flourishing universities. Where Protestantism was established many of these universities quickly fell into decay. The universities of Erfurt and Rostoch, amongst others, were entirely ruined.

The Reformation produced analogous results in Denmark, Norway, and Sweden. In 1594 the governing senate of Copenhagen addressed a circular to the bishops of the kingdom, in order to call their attention to certain measures which they judged necessary to arrest the ruin of learning, "which it could not be denied was imminent." "Village schools existed no longer," says Döllinger. "Even in towns, schools for the people, as well as those of a higher class, were in a state of complete decay during the sixteenth century."‡ It is well

---
* Loc. cit. p. 400. † *Ib.* p. 401.
‡ *Die Reformation*, etc., tom. xi. p. 660. Heart-rending accounts are met with in Döllinger of the intellectual and moral state of Denmark at this epoch.

known that in Sweden the change of religion was violently brought about by the king, Gustavus Vasa, whose chief object was to gain possession of Church property in order to pay the debts he had contracted by his wars. In this country, as in Denmark, the pernicious influence of the Reformation affected, in the first instance, schools and public instruction. We may see this from two letters, bearing date 1533 and 1540, addressed by the king to his subjects at Upsala, Westeras, and the provinces of Upland and Indermania: "We are convinced, and we make known to you," says the king, "that the schools in all towns of our kingdom are in a deplorable state of decay; to such a point that, in those schools where there were formerly three hundred students, scarcely fifty can now be reckoned. In many parishes they are completely deserted, which must be highly prejudicial to the kingdom. The principal cause of this state of things is that you, good, honest people that you are, neglect to have your children instructed as you were accustomed to do formerly, and that you will not assist poor scholars as is your duty, and as your fathers and ancestors did.* Besides, but a very small number of subjects are now destined to pursue learning; and those who devote themselves, or wish to devote themselves, to it are now obliged to

---

* Gustavus Vasa forgot that he had himself given the death-blow to learning when he confiscated the property of the Church, and employed it for far different objects than the education of youth.

give it up for want of means and support on your part. . . . The refusal or reduction of tithes and other duties of the same kind has had the fatal effect of diminishing the means of maintenance formerly granted to those who frequented the schools; and as, moreover, the title of student or minister is now held in disesteem, few parents will consent to devote their children to learning, so that shortly this country will be but indifferently provided with learned and capable men."*

In a letter to the Bishop of Osnaburgh, the Senator Joeran Gylte writes, "that public instruction is in so deplorable a state in Sweden that a new state of barbarism was to be feared; that he knew but ten preachers, or high functionaries of the Church, who could really be considered learned; and that, in the whole kingdom, it would not be easy to find a single theologian or physician who had attained the degree of doctor."†

Erasmus, who was a competent judge of the state of literature and science, points out the disastrous influence exercised upon learning by the new doctrines in several passages of his writings. Especially he denounces Luther as the chief author of the decay of instruction. He says: "When a man professes, as Luther did, that the Aristotelian philosophy—that is to say, all philosophical science based upon the principles of Aristotle—is but the work of Satan; when he looks upon all speculative science

* Ap. Döllinger, loc. cit. p. 664.   † *Ibid.* p. 668.

in general as sin and error; when, with Farell, he treats openly and on all occasions every kind of human knowledge as the conception of hell and the devil, how can any one suppose that such principles should produce aught but a contempt for study, and the predominance of avaricious and sensual passions? Has it not been openly taught, at Strasburg and elsewhere, that it is contrary to the spirit of the Gospel that people should lose their time, whether in studying ancient languages (Hebrew alone excepted) or in instructing themselves in any other branch of human learning?"*

Surely this will suffice. Is it not evident that Protestantism announced itself to Europe, not as the emancipator of reason and science, as some pretend, but as the inauguration of a veritable barbarism? The Reformation of the sixteenth century appears in history as a revolt of the senses, and of all that is low and vile in human nature, against reason and moral dignity. It is the resurrection of pagan materialism, with its debasement and infamy, as far as the spiritual atmosphere which long centuries of Christianity had generated in Europe would permit. Had Protestant nations followed literally the teaching of Luther and his accomplices, they would have sunk below even pagan vileness;

* *Epist. ad Fratres Germaniæ infer.* p. 4. Coloniæ, 1561.—*Epist. Londini,* 1642, p. 984. " Typographi narrant," says the same Erasmus in a letter, " se ante hoc Evangelium citius distrahere solitos tria voluminum millia, quam nunc distrahant sexcenta." And again, elsewhere, " Ubicumque regnat Lutheranismus, ibi litterarum est interitus."

for pagans did not anathematize either reason or liberty, and Athens and Rome honored science, literature, and art. The people were devoured by the most ignoble practical materialism; but the philosophers, at all events, glorified reason, and exalted noble and generous actions. The moral temperament of European nations was strong enough, thank God, to resist, in part if not completely, the debasing doctrines proclaimed by the chiefs of Protestantism. Soon a number of Protestants might be seen, who, alarmed at the flood of depravity which threatened to overwhelm civilization with its unclean waters, began to work courageously at opposing a dike to the devastating torrent. They strove to correct what was too visibly base in the new religion, and to assimilate themselves as much as possible to the moral teaching of the Catholic Church, whose neighborhood was not without influence upon them. But, after all, it is a fact taught by history that Protestantism, as set forth by its originators, bears manifestly the mark of the beast, and that it is the negation of all those principles which constitute the strength and honor of European civilization.

We know what was the attitude assumed by the Catholic Church in the face of this revolution which threatened to destroy all moral order. She publicly condemned the mad doctrines of Luther and his competitors; she solemnly anathematized the two fundamental articles of the Protestant creed, namely, that reason has lost all power in that which regards the moral order, and that liberty no longer exists.* She maintained the prerogatives of reason and human liberty with immovable firmness, and upheld the rights of morality against the attacks of pretended reformers. She thus saved not only revealed but natural religion, and with it all those notions of right, duty, justice, dignity, responsibility, moral greatness, without which nations, as well as individuals, must fall into contempt and decay, and which raise the standard of civilization in proportion to the influence they exercise upon society.

By the admirable laws of the Council of Trent in matters of discipline, the Catholic Church opposed a true, serious, Christian reformation to the false, cynical reformation of Luther and his accomplices. The Council of Trent appears as the bulwark not only of the Christian Faith, but of reason, justice, morality, and civilization.

And whilst proud, corrupt men, assuming to be reformers of the Church, were denying reason, denouncing science, and ruining schools of learning, a new Religious Order came forth from the ever-fruitful bosom of the Church, which was destined to struggle with incomparable glory against the moral and intellectual barbarism with which these strange reformers threatened Europe. The Company of Jesus, illustrious from its very birth, established schools in all directions, founded missions,

---

* See the Council of Trent, Sess. vi.

The Principal Causes of Infidelity. 105

and combated, with a zeal which can never be sufficiently admired, the prevailing state of ignorance and immorality.

We must now say a few words of the general principle on which Protestantism is based, and point out the fruits produced by it.

SECTION II.

The Negative Principle of Protestantism, or the Rejection of Authority in Matters of Religion—Fanaticism and Rationalism the twofold Fruit of this Principle.

WHEN the assailants of the Catholic Faith hail Protestantism as the liberator of reason and science, they certainly cannot intend to speak of the positive and peculiar doctrines of the Reformation of the sixteenth century; for, as we have seen, these doctrines sacrificed reason to a blind and impossible faith. Apparently they considered only the general principle of the Reformation, which consists definitively in the rejection of all authority in matters of religion. When Luther revolted against the authority of the Pope, he naturally sought to justify his revolt; and he certainly did this most effectually when he declared that, according to the true spirit of Christianity, each Christian is the judge of religious truth, that he is independent of all external authority, and that the Bible is his sole guide. Hence arose the principle which was to serve as the foundation of Protestantism: it was the offspring of the pride of a monk who sought to legitimatize his want of submission, and his revolt against authority. Luther had no suspicion of the lengths to which the principle he proclaimed would be carried; and it must be admitted that most Protestant sects recognize its value only so far as it affects the authority of the Pope: they are ready to accept any authority, provided it is not the authority of the Pope. But logic preserves its rights, and sooner or later the consequences involved in a principle will make themselves felt. The natural consequence of the Protestant principle was fanaticism or rationalism, according as religious enthusiasm or mere individual reason might prevail in the reading and interpretation of the Bible. Fanaticism, and fanaticism of the most extravagant kind, showed itself in the earliest stages of the Reformation.

"Protestantism had existed but five years," says Möhler, "when several inhabitants of Zwickau, Nicholas Storch, Mark Thomas, Mark Stalmer, Thomas Muneer, Martin Cellarius, and others, repaired to Wittemburg in order to confer with the doctors who had adorned the birthplace of Gospel

Truth. As Luther was then at Wartburg, it devolved on Melancthon to receive them. These brethren in Christ were sent by the Holy Ghost: revelations had been made to them on various subjects, but for the present they contented themselves with attacking the baptism of infants, which they rejected as contrary to Holy Scripture."* Thus arose the sect of Anabaptists. Now that the authority of the Church was set at naught, and all doctrinal guidance rejected, each man understood the Scripture in his own fashion, and was but too ready to mistake his own fancies for the inspirations of the Holy Spirit; and all the more because religious activity in man was denied in principle, and he was regarded as passive under the hand of God. How many visionaries were to be found among the first disciples of Luther!† And would to God that these fanatics had been no more than extravagant visionaries! But with many fanaticism became the source of the most atrocious cruelties and most frightful disorders. Germany was inundated with torrents of blood. Not to mention other facts, the peasants' war, kindled by Luther's doctrines and stirred into a flame by the fanaticism of the Anabaptists, covered the soil with thousands of human hecatombs. One historian says that, during this savage war, "more than a hundred

---

* *Symbolik*, b. ii. ch. i. † See Balmez, tom. i. p. 258, etc.

thousand men might be reckoned as killed on the battle-fields of Germany, seven cities were dismantled, a thousand Monasteries razed to the ground, three hundred Churches burnt, and immense treasures of painting, sculpture, glass, and engraving were destroyed."* Who is ignorant of the immoral and bloody follies of which Munster was the theatre under the tyranny of Mathias Harlem and John of Leyden, that tailor who was crowned King of Sion, on the 24th of June, 1534?

Rationalism was another result of the rejection of the authority of the Church. Very shortly after Luther's revolt Protestants began in earnest to make use of the principle of free examination, and to apply it to the interpretation of the Bible and the discussion of the Christian Faith. These men did not believe, with Luther and the other fanatics of whom we have just spoken, that reason was extinct, and that it had been replaced by the Holy Spirit; but instead of understanding Scripture in conformity with tradition and the authority of the Church, they recognized no other rule for the interpretation of Holy Scripture than human reason, and soon went so far as to pretend that nothing is evident in Scripture except what does not exceed the measure of reason. On these grounds was

* Rohrbacher, *Histoire Universelle de l'Eglise Catholique*, t. xxiii. p. 227.

based Socinianism, whose principles were definitively established by Faustus Socinus, in the second half of the sixteenth century. Poland was at first the principal theatre of this sect.* Its followers accept Holy Scripture as the source of Divine Revelation; but they pretend that God has revealed no dogma superior to human reason, and whenever they meet with the declaration of a doctrine in the Bible which is above reason they interpret the text in a metaphorical or allegorical sense. All the Christian mysteries were soon suppressed. Socinianism was the first rough draught of Rationalism.

Socinian ideas quickly found a number of supporters among learned Protestants in Germany, France, and England. Various Protestant sects, who appealed to the Bible by the same right and with the same authority, were soon divided on all points of doctrine. They were agreed only on the two articles—there is one God, and Jesus Christ is the Messiah. They were constrained to restrict the fundamental and essential dogmas of Christianity to these two articles, under pain of condemning the principle whence all these contradictions sprang. And we must observe that whilst they acknowledged Jesus Christ as the Messiah, they did not intend to prejudge the question as to whether he were God or

* Lilius and Faustus Socinus, who gave their names to this sect, lived long in Poland, where they made numerous proselytes.

merely a messenger from God. Reduced to these proportions, Christianity evidently lost all supernatural character, and became nothing more than a timid Deism. Thus it appears in the *Reasonable Christianity* of Locke, and other writings of a similar class.*

The door was opened to infidelity. Protestantism was beginning to bear fruit.

* The historical development of the Protestant principle is given in detail in the work entitled *De Methodo Theologiæ*, p. 117, by Laforêt.

CHAPTER VII.

Modern Infidelity—Infidelity prevails first in England, afterward in France and Germany—Poverty of the Infidel Philosophy of the Eighteenth Century—Theological Infidelity in Germany.

INFIDELS are to be met with in every century of the Christian era; but such a spectacle as we have had before our eyes during the last two centuries was never witnessed from the day in which Christianity first took possession of the nations of Europe. Infidelity has become a power, and a formidable power, possessing a whole army of soldiers. Here is a singular phenomenon in the annals of the Christian world. Protestantism, as we have just seen, was one chief cause of this grievous fact. By the logical development of the principle born of Luther's revolt, Protestantism led directly to Rationalism; but in another way—in an indirect way, it contributed to the triumph of infidelity by diminishing the action of the Catholic Church, and by weakening in a degree hitherto unknown the religious spirit in Europe. Infidelity first displayed its power on a Protestant soil

—in England. In the year 1624, Lord Herbert, of Cherbury, published a work in which Deism was set forth and systematically defended. The empire of opinion in England was conquered for unbelief by Hobbes, Toland, Blount, Shaftesbury, Tindal, Morgan, Chubb, Collins, Woolston, and Bolingbroke. Bolingbroke was the master of Voltaire. It is well known that the French infidels of the eighteenth century were but the echoes of English Deists. M. Villemain recognizes and proves this fact in his *Cours de Littérature Française.* He says, "The boldest arguments of French philosophy in the eighteenth century may be found in the English school of the beginning of that century." That philosophy was summed up in Bolingbroke. In his dissipated youth, his high official station under Queen Anne, and in his exile, he gave himself up to the pursuit of an anti-Christian erudition. His singular learning charmed and perplexed Voltaire in the conversations they held together in Touraine.* There, in place of the libertine scepticism which had been his first school, and the only philosophy of Vendôme and Chaulieu, he met with a learned polyglot infidelity, based on the authority of a philosopher and a statesman. We can easily conceive how vast must have been the power

* When Bolingbroke was banished from England by Act of Parliament, he withdrew into France, and had a magnificent residence in Touraine. He returned to England in 1726.

The Principal Causes of Infidelity. 113

exercised by the reflection of this erudition, the confidence of this bold scepticism, the essence of irreligion exhaled by such a multitude of books read rapidly by Voltaire, and imported into France, where the *douane* was powerless to stop them, and there was no moral influence to resist their power.* Voltaire followed Bolingbroke to England, and passed three years with the leaders of English infidelity. " Diderot, the most active mind of the eighteenth century after Voltaire, borrowed his first philosophical studies, and his first essay of the *Encyclopedia*, from England.† Rousseau took a great portion of his ideas on politics and education,‡ and Condillac all his philosophy, from Locke." § Condillac was not himself an unbeliever, but his philosophy, a pale reflection, as it was, of Locke's, opened the way to all the degradation of materialism. It is curious to hear this poor Abbé de Condillac, the oracle of the infidel philosophers of the eighteenth century, date the advent of philosophy in the modern world from Bacon and Locke, whilst he counts

---

* Tableau du dix-huitième siècle, V⁵ leç.

† Diderot and D'Alembert, the editors of the *Encyclopedia*, inscribed the name of Francis Bacon on the frontispiece of this famous work, and brought out this sad monument of the French science of the eighteenth century under the auspices of the English Chancellor.

‡ Locke's *Essay on Civil Government* formed a model for the *Contrat Social* of Rousseau, and to his *Thoughts upon Education* Rousseau is largely indebted for his *Emile*.

§ Villemain, loc. cit. IV⁵ leç.

for nothing Descartes, Malebranche, Leibnitz, Bossuet, Fénélon—all the great minds of the seventeenth century, who* are the eternal glory of French literature.* I have said elsewhere, making use of Condillac's sacramental formula in his explanation of the generation of faculties in his statue, that Condillacism is philosophy changing itself into nonsense.† I am certain that this sentence will not now be disputed by any serious philosopher, whether he be a believer or an unbeliever. Locke is certainly not strong in metaphysics; the heights to which the genius of Malebranche, Leibnitz, Bossuet, and Fénélon soars are inaccessible to him; but Locke is an eagle compared to Condillac. Yet every one knows that Condillac held the sceptre of philosophy in France even up to the first years of the present century, and for fifty years the contemners of the Christian Faith bowed before this man. This does not prove the progress of reason. It appears to me that if, instead of seeking inspiration from England, the France of the eighteenth century had been faithful to herself by following up the philosophical and literary traditions of her seventeenth century, reason would not have been the loser.

* See Condillac's *Introduction de l'Essai sur l'Origine des Connaissances Humaines.* Leibnitz wrote his two great philosophical works, his *Essais de Théodicée* and his *Nouveaux Essais sur l'Entendement Humain*, in French.
† *Revue Catholique de Louvain.* 1863.

Oh! that men who look upon infidelity as the natural and necessary result of the legitimate progress of reason would draw a simple comparison, but a comparison which speaks most eloquently. The seventeenth century, as represented by her greatest men, was thoroughly Christian; the eighteenth, on the contrary, was infidel. Now, which is the greater of these two centuries for power of reason, extent of science, and brilliancy of literature? I think among earnest men there cannot be two opinions on the subject: the seventeenth century is undoubtedly far superior in all these respects to the eighteenth.*

As to philosophy, which is the highest manifestation of reason, we must admit that among French infidels of the eighteenth century it was entirely null. Who in the present day would dream of taking Helvetius, D'Holbach, Lamettrie, and other thinkers of the same school, inheritors of Condillac's sensualism, for philosophers? What philosopher would consent to speak seriously of the pretended philosophy of Voltaire and J. J. Rousseau? They were writers of genius, I admit, but

* "The *great* writers of the age of Louis XIV.," says Maine de Biran, "were so only in their own estimation; this no longer exists, and now the most brilliant amongst them seem but as monkeys, whose tricks excite our surprise; they are lively, nothing more. . . . I see men of wit who believe only in themselves; they are puffed up with pride, completely satisfied with their own utterances; they imagine the world admires them, and in fact this self-esteem gains for them the approbation of men of weak judgment: competent judges ridicule them and their pretensions."—Maine de Biran, *Sa Vie et ses Pensées*, p. 329.

strangers alike to philosophy and to all science properly so-called. They were men of letters, but neither philosophers nor scholars. If, then, the eighteenth century was infidel, it evidently did not become so by its intellectual and scientific superiority. We must seek elsewhere for the causes of that unbelief, which, with frightful rapidity, invaded the higher ranks of French society and spread thence over the rest of Europe.

A conscientious and learned man, the Abbé Bergier, who lived in the midst of the infidels of the last century, and read all their works, has not been afraid to affirm that their unbelief had no other source than licentiousness and the unbridled sway of the passions. "We make a point," he says, at the beginning of his *Traité de la Vraie Religion*, " of ignoring whether the authors of the crowd of impious books which attack religion, are living or dead, fellow-countrymen or foreigners, known or unknown; we would depict them only by their writings: we attack books, not men. We will only mention by name those whose works are generally avowed, and we will allege no other facts than those which result from the works themselves. Limiting ourselves to this irrefragable proof, we maintain that licentiousness and unbridled passion are the real causes of infidelity."*

The Baron d'Holbach, who, in his capacity of

---

* Introd. § 14.

The Principal Causes of Infidelity. 117

first maître d'hôtel of philosophy,* must have been well acquainted with the philosophical or infidel party, passes the following judgment on the greater number of his accomplices, in a book of mournful celebrity : " We must allow that corruption of manners, debauchery, license, and even frivolity of mind may often lead to irreligion or infidelity. . . . Many people give up prejudices they had adopted through vanity and hearsay; these pretended freethinkers have examined nothing for themselves, they rely on others whom they suppose to have weighed matters more carefully. How can men, given up to voluptuousness and debauchery, plunged in excess, ambitious, intriguing, frivolous, and dissipated—or depraved women of wit and fashion—how can such as these be capable of forming an opinion of a religion they have never thoroughly examined, of feeling the force of an argument, or of embracing a system in all its parts ?" †

About the same period another leader of unbe-

---

* D'Holbach was in the habit of giving two dinners a week to his friends the philosophers. The Abbé Galiani, writing to him from Naples, the 7th April, 1770, says, " La philosophie dont vous êtes le premier maître d'hôtel, mange-t-elle toujours d'aussi bon appétit ? " It suffices to make the most glorious titles odious that a certain man should have appropriated them. The name of sophist, so honorable in its origin, was for ever disgraced by Gorgias, Protagoras, and other buffoons whose notions were so cruelly lashed by the irony of Socrates. It is not the fault of Voltaire's school that philosophy did not share the same fate.

† *Système de la Nature*, tom. ii. ch. 13. *Le Système de la Nature* is a manual of atheism.

lief spoke thus of a multitude of infidels: "Can philosophy boast of having for adherents, in a dissolute nation, a multitude of dissipated and licentious libertines who despise a gloomy and false religion on hearsay, without knowledge of the duties they ought to substitute for it? Will philosophy be flattered by the interested homage and stupid applause of a troop of voluptuaries, of public robbers, of intemperate and licentious men, who conclude that because they forget their God and despise his worship, therefore they owe nothing to themselves or to society, and who think themselves wise, because (though often with fear and remorse) they trample under foot chimeras which compelled them to respect decency and morality?"*

Helvetius admits that his friends, the leaders of infidelity, were sometimes more taken up with the correction of their work than of their behavior.† Who is ignorant that Voltaire and Rousseau were not precisely models of chastity nor even of probity? Frederick II., who had long been intimately acquainted with Voltaire, and who was certainly not very exacting on the score of morals, wrote thus to Dargot: "Voltaire behaved here like a consummate scoundrel and cheat, and I paid him off as he deserves. He is a wretch, and for the honor of genius I am sorry that a man who has so much should be so full of mischief. Voltaire is

* *Essai sur les Préjuges*, ch. 8.
† *De l'Esprit*, 2 discours, c. 9.

the most wicked fool I have ever known: is only good to read. You cannot imagine what duplicity, cheating, and villany he practised here."*

There is no doubt that corruption of morals, joined to the weakening of Christian sentiments which Protestantism had brought about in Europe, was the principal cause of the infidelity of the eighteenth century. Reason and science had nothing to do with it. I believe that no honest man, who has read some of the writings of the most eminent infidels of that period, and who is acquainted with their moral history, will dispute the fact.

But let me not be misunderstood. I do not mean to say that moral corruption is the sole cause of infidelity: unbelief has many other sources, and I freely acknowledge that among infidels men are to be found whose lives are purer than the lives of many Christians. I merely recall a historical fact which is indisputable.

Further, two distinct forms of infidelity are met with in the eighteenth century. By the side of that frivolous infidelity, which for the most part originated and was kept up in the immoral atmosphere of the *salons* of the Voltairian school, there was a serious, earnest infidelity, produced by

* The work of M. Nicolardot, *Ménage et Finances de Voltaire, avec une introduction sur les mœurs des cours et des salons au xviii. siècle*, Paris, 1854, shows what were the habits of Voltaire and the philosophers of the eighteenth century. I do not approve the general tone of this work, but it contains some curious information.

causes of a totally different kind. This serious infidelity prevailed in Germany especially, and its principal organs were the Protestant theologians. Germany had paid a heavy tribute to the raillery and frivolity which distinguished French infidelity. Frederick II., who had an equal contempt for morality and religion, had made Berlin the rendezvous of French free-thinkers, and encouraged them in their work of demoralization. The spirit of the French school was exactly represented by some German writers, such as Edelmann, Bahrdt, and Basedow. But about the same period a grave, earnest Rationalism arose from a wholly different source. The Protestant theologian, Semler, carrying out to its legitimate conclusion the principle of free examination in the interpretation of Holy Scripture, founded theological or exegetical Rationalism. This new form of infidelity soon found numerous supporters in the ranks of the Protestant clergy, and since the beginning of the century it has been dominant in the theological schools of Protestantism.

We know that with Protestants theology rests wholly and exclusively on the Bible. Luther, and the companions of his revolt against the traditional authority of the Catholic Church, pretended that the Bible was the sole source of Divine Revelation, and that all Christian doctrine was most clearly declared in it; that, consequently, it was useless to interrogate tradition, which, besides, had for the most part only corrupted the purity of the teaching contained in Holy Scripture. Hence the boasted disdain of the early Protestants for tradition and its most venerable interpreters, the Fathers and Doctors of the Church. Protestant theology knows only the Bible, and is in fact but the mere simple interpretation of the Bible: it is confounded with the exegesis itself. Now, to the greater number of Protestant theologians the Bible is but a book like any other, stripped of all supernatural character, and no more representing a Divine teaching than the dialogues of Plato or the metaphysics of Aristotle. They interpret it as a purely human work; and when they meet with facts or doctrines which transcend the powers of nature or the capacity of reason, they either reject them altogether or explain them so as to bring them down to the level of the purely natural order. This is the rationalistic exegesis, which is at the same time theological rationalism. It is a rationalism which rests, at least in appearance, on the Bible, and makes its comments with the greatest care; but in reality it robs the Bible of its very essence, and recognizes no other light than that of mere human reason. It differs from ordinary or philosophical rationalism only in form.

For some years past, a movement favorable to the Christian Faith has stirred the ranks of the Protestant theologians of Germany. Many distinguished scholars have broken with rationalism. Unfortunately their faith has no fixed rule, and their opinions are, for the most part, vague and uncertain. The early Protestants, in practice, forgot the principle of free examination and free interpretation of the Bible, and were fixed in their belief by common and supposed obligatory confessions of Faith: now, even believing theologians no longer accept these ancient creeds. Julius Müller says: "It is patent, that in all the theological works recently published, and in which the collective doctrines to be believed are set forth, there is not one which has not declared that the Lutheran confessions need modification on some point or other;* and this regards definitions of the highest importance." And Ehrenberg said, before the general Synod of Berlin, that he had for years sought a man who should agree on all points with his *Confessions of Faith*, and that he had never found such a one. It is affirmed that, for the last hundred years, no theologian, either from his professor's chair or from the pulpit, has taught one single doctrine perfectly agreeing in form and matter with the published *Confessions*. † How can a common settled faith be maintained, when no doctrinal authority is recognized on religious subjects? Would that those theologians who believe and who must groan over the divisions and uncertainty pro-

* *Deutsche Zeitschrift*, 1855, p. 107.
† *Revue mensuelle pour l'Eglise évangélique unie*. 1847, ii. 84. Ap. Döllinger, *L'Eglise et les Eglises*, pp. 308, 309. Paris, 1862.

duced by the necessary development of the principles of the Reformation — would that they might at length comprehend that the authority of the Catholic Church is the Divine, indispensable safeguard of the firmness and unity of the Christian Faith, and that a full, pure Faith is to be found in the bosom of Catholicism alone!

CHAPTER VIII.

The Principal Forms of Contemporary Infidelity— Materialism —Pantheism— Sophistry and Scepticism—Spiritualistic Rationalism.

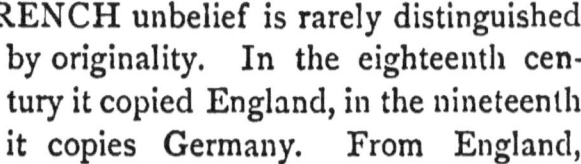RENCH unbelief is rarely distinguished by originality. In the eighteenth century it copied England, in the nineteenth it copies Germany. From England, France borrowed that cynical deism and debased philosophy which quickly engendered materialism; from Germany she has in our days received Pantheism, and that presumptuous sophistry which, together with the principles of religion, pretend also to change the fundamental laws of reason itself.

How thankful and happy should believers feel when they behold the result of the arrogant efforts of poor human reason in revolt against the teaching of Christian Faith! For the last century two systems have been predominant by turns in the schools of infidelity; and what are these systems? Materialism and Pantheism. And what is Materialism? what is Pantheism? I ask the question of every understanding that is not dead or wholly perverted by falsehood. Materialism is reason abdicating her throne, which she abandons to the flesh; it is the mind compassing its own ruin, and delivering itself up as a vile slave to the caprices of the body which was made to serve it; it is the soul losing the very consciousness of its own reality, and believing itself to be but the property or a dependent of the organs of sense; it is man assimilated to the brutes, and glorying in this assimilation. And what is Pantheism? Pantheism, as we shall explain presently, is reason abdicating its throne and abandoning it to sophistry; it is the radical change of all principles which form the light of the moral and intellectual life of humanity; it is the negation of good sense and reason—of pure, simple reason—that which all men call reason. Behold the intellectual and moral progress accomplished by the human mind in revolt against God! What a lesson for any one capable of reflecting and judging!

At the beginning of the present century, Materialism was the fashionable doctrine with infidels, at least in France. We know to what a depth of degradation and ignominy it had sunk at the end of the last century. Men, who in their pride despised the Christian Faith, and rejected Christianity in the name of the progress of reason, blushed not to place a naked prostitute upon the altar of the Incarnate God. Behold the goddess, who, by a just judgment of Divine Providence, was permitted to call herself the goddess of reason!

Materialism was vigorously combated by men whose names have retained their celebrity. Royer, Collard, Maine de Biran, M. Cousin, carried on a persevering war against this ignoble philosophy, which ended in destroying its authority as a recognized philosophical system. Many unbelievers, however, renounced Materialism only to embrace Pantheism. France and Europe are indebted to Germany for this monstrous philosophy.

The earliest professors of Pantheism in modern times were Giordano Bruno, an unfrocked monk of the sixteenth century, and Baruch Spinoza, a Dutch Jew, of the seventeenth. As long as the mind of Europe preserved its uprightness and balance, there was nothing to fear from Pantheism. The seventeenth century only beheld in Spinoza's philosophy the mad dream of a delirious mind; the eighteenth century, though infidel, borrowed nothing from Spinoza's philosophy, and took from him only a portion of his rationalistic criticism of the Bible.* Pantheism established itself in Europe, and began to acquire importance only in the last years of the eighteenth century, and especially in the beginning of the nineteenth. It appeared first in Germany, where, thanks to the religious decomposition brought about by the natural development of Protestantism, the training of the intellect had passed

* Voltaire and his followers were only acquainted with the *Traité Théologico-Politico* of Spinoza; they were ignorant of *L'Ethique*, which contains this writer's philosophy.

almost wholly into the hands of the rationalistic philosophy. Kant was at that time its great master. This philosopher, who had been thrown into an absurd course by the Cartesian formalism of Wolf, made the idea of God, and all those general and absolute ideas which are the light and rule of reason, purely subjective forms of the human mind —necessary forms certainly, but devoid of all objective value. Thence he argued the impossibility of proving the existence of God, and the reality of a moral order beyond our *ego*, by means of *theoretical reason*, that is to say, of reason properly so-called. Johann Gottlieb Fichte, the most celebrated of the disciples of the philosopher of Königsberg, went still further. He taught that there is no real God, no moral order exterior to the *ego;* according to Fichte it is this *ego* which is God, which is the true Sovereign Reality; all else is the work of the activity of this *ego*, the product of thought. This is idealistic or subjective Pantheism, and was the first form of the revived Pantheism.

Pantheism having reappeared, the works of Spinoza, which had been long forgotten, became once more the fashion; and this writer, who professes the most brutal and repulsive materialistic Pantheism, was hailed as the prince of modern philosophy. Infidel France soon shared the infatuation of Germany for this miserable philosopher whom Malebranche called a wretch, and whose system he treated as a frightful chimera. I want no other proof of the feebleness and decline of reason among our infidel philosophers than their judgment of Spinoza.

Schelling and Hegel were the most famous representatives of Pantheism in Germany during the first half of the present century. Hegel is the undoubted master of the sophistry of our day.

Victor Cousin, the founder of the eclectic school, who, in 1817, visited the leaders of the philosophical movement in Germany, imported Pantheism into France. For several years past he has sincerely repudiated this fatal doctrine. The most considerable writers of the eclectic school never adopted Pantheism. But by the side of this purely philosophical school arose another whose teachers openly professed that system. I speak of the humanitarian socialist school, which reckons Pierre Leroux among its leaders, as also the unhappy Abbé de Lamennais, whose pride plunged him into every kind of error. Leroux teaches Pantheism clearly in his work *De l'Humanité*, and Lamennais tried to reconcile it with Christianity in *L'Esquisse d'une Philosophie*. A philosopher of some repute, M. Vacherot, formerly a disciple of Cousin, still professes Pantheism. M. Renan lately summed up the metaphysics of Vacherot in the following sentence: "God is the idea of the world, and the world is the reality of God." As for M. Renan himself, that tardy copyist of German extravagance, he recognizes no God but the ideal, as it manifests itself in the human mind, with which it is confounded. This is pure atheism.*

Belgium did not escape the general contagion. A German philosopher, M. Ahrens, a disciple of Krause, introduced Pantheism into the University of Brussels. It is now professed there by M. Tiberghien, the pupil and successor of M. Ahrens, in the chair of philosophy.

This detestable system has assumed many various forms, and I willingly admit that the Pantheism of Schelling, Krause, and other contemporary philosophers differs in many respects from the Pantheism of Spinoza; but these differences are but accessory; the foundation of the system is the same in all, and it is this : Pantheism consists in recognizing but one sole substance, and in giving to this one substance the name of God. God is all, since all participates of his substance, and is truly consubstantial with him. According to this doctrine, God is no longer a personal Being, subsisting in himself, and living by his own life, substantially distinct from the world and from each one of us, a Being gifted with a personal intelligence and will. He is the sole and universal substance, displaying himself under the form of the world, and of hu-

* The *Vie de Jésus*, which the infidel press of Belgium, France, and Italy has welcomed as the last utterance of German criticism, has excited irrepressible ridicule in learned Germany, even in the bosom of the rationalistic schools. Grave German critics cannot comprehend how any one, in the critical state of science, can regard in a serious light the author of such a book.

manity, developing himself necessarily and unceasingly under this twofold form, which is the sole and necessary manifestation of his life. God exists not without the world and without man; he has no reality but in them and by them; man and the world are in strict terms the realization of God. This is the essence of all Pantheism. We maintain that such a doctrine not only injures reason, but radically destroys it. Nothing can be plainer.

Pantheism, by recognizing only one sole substance or essence, called by the name of God, pretends, and must pretend, that all things and all ideas are fundamentally identical, and can only differ in form; it proclaims the principle of absolute and universal ideality. Hence the identity of God and the world, of mind and matter, of necessity and liberty, of truth and falsehood, of good and evil, of just and unjust, of being and not being, as Hegel teaches positively: hence in one word the identity of things that are contrary and contradictory. All this is the direct denial of that fundamental principle without which there is neither reason, language, nor thought. It is impossible to affirm yes and no at the same time with regard to the same point. I ask, is not all this the total, radical destruction of reason? No, Pantheism is not philosophy; it is mere sophistry; it is the production of a reason overthrown and become unreason or systematic folly.

The logic of Hegel, in which that daring master

of German philosophy affirms in express terms the identity of things that are contrary and contradictory, is simply the logic of supreme absurdity, and it is the only logic that Pantheism can produce.*

Observe further that by representing God, or the universal substance, as something indeterminate, which according to Hegel's expression becomes and never is, which changes and modifies itself unceasingly, which develops itself and progresses indefinitely, Pantheism suppresses at one stroke those necessary, inimitable, absolute ideas which are the support, light, and rule of our intelligence, and without which man is no longer a reasonable being, *rationis particeps*. If there be no perfect and unchangeable God, how can there be unchangeable truth? Where would truth have her foundation or her abode? Consequently how could there be principles? With the immutability of God, all truths and all principles must necessarily fall. No longer is anything fixed, all is subject to change. All, according to the saying of Heracli-

---

* Pius IX., in his memorable allocution of June 9th, 1862, thus characterizes Pantheism: "With a dishonesty only equalled by egregious folly, they do not hesitate to assert that there exists no divine Being, no eternal providence, omniscient and supreme, distinct from the universe, and that God and nature are identical, and that God as a consequence is subject to change; that all things are God and have the very essence of the Deity, that God is identical with the world, and necessarily spirit with matter, necessity with liberty, truth with falsehood, good with evil, what is just with injustice; than which it is certainly impossible to invent or imagine anything more foolish, more impious, more contrary to reason itself."

tus, is in perpetual flow. In this universal and incessant movement, in which at every instant one wave succeeds another wave, reason can no longer exist, and thought, deprived of its anchor, wanders at hazard over a tempest-tossed ocean.

This is the goal attained by that proud philosophy which the most famous infidels of the nineteenth century have thought fit to substitute, in the name of progress and reason, for the ancient Christian Faith.

For some time past Pantheism has lost ground in Europe; it is on the decline in strictly philosophical schools, though it undoubtedly still reckons a great number of adherents in Germany, Belgium, France, and elsewhere. And it is unfortunately undeniable that the influence of Pantheism will be long felt among us. This detestable philosophy has corrupted all principles, and the reason of Europe has probably suffered irreparable injury from the long sway which it has exercised over the minds of men. The manner in which many writers who do not profess Pantheism treat religion, social and moral sciences, history, and even literature, sufficiently attests that they still suffer from this fatal influence.

Since the decline of Pantheism in Germany, Materialism has gained favor there. At present, it numbers many supporters among the representatives of philosophy, but especially among the interpreters of the natural sciences. Feuerbach, Max Stirner, Arnold Ruge, Vogt, Moleschott,

L. Büchner,* not to mention others, reject everything that transcends the limits of experience—God, the moral law, the immortality of the soul, all general principles which together form the light and rule of reason, and without which man is no longer a reasonable being, but a mere sensitive being, an animal. German Materialism followed Pantheism, and in more than one instance sprang directly from it. Hegel deified man: his disciple, Feuerbach, brought man down to the level of the beasts. Is not this a repetition, in the moral order, of the old story of Nabuchodonosor? Man madly lifts himself up to the desire of becoming God, then falls below his own nature of man; he becomes like to the beasts, and sinks so low as even to seek to convince himself that such ignominy is his glory.

In France, two or three writers calling themselves philosophers have, in the name of reason, resumed the defence of Materialism. Auguste Comte and Littré have founded a pretended philosophy which they adorn with the name of positive philosophy, because it recognizes only facts attested

---

* Moleschott's book, *Le Cours Circulaire de la Vie*, (*Kreislauf des Lebens,*) published for the first time in 1852, has passed through four editions in ten years; Büchner's, entitled *Matière et Force*, (*Kraft und Stoff,*) which appeared in 1856, has had seven editions in five years; it has been translated into French. M. Charles Vogt, in a work recently published under the title *Leçons sur l'Homme, sa Place dans la Création et dans l'Histoire de la Terre*, tells us that "lecerveau sécrète la pensée, comme le foie sécrète la bile et les reins sécrète l'urine." This is the pure teaching of Cabanis.

by experience. The school which proudly calls itself the critical school is worthy to figure by the side of the positivist school. Taine and Renan, who are firmly persuaded that before the appearance of their school there was neither science nor philosophy upon earth, are its chief upholders. These enlightened minds profess Materialism, Taine roughly and openly, Renan in delicate terms, and with shades of such nicety and variety as to do honor to his imagination. This austere moralist brands that "egotism which makes us eagerly seek the reward of virtue beyond the tomb."* In M. Renan's eyes the immortality of the soul is a chimera which fades away before the touch of criticism, it is an invention of Greek philosophy. This eminent critic mocks at the "doctrine, called spiritualist, which cuts man into two parts, body and soul, and looks upon it as quite natural, that while the body rots the soul should survive."† In fact, is it not much more natural that the soul should decay with the body?

What a noble philosophy! And how proud ought a man to feel who has made such wonderful discoveries! M. Renan is, in fact, so enchanted with himself, that—in order doubtless to justify his immeasurable pride—he goes so far as to point out pride and disdain as the chief among

---

* *Vie de Jésus*, p. 55. Paris, 1863. † *Ib.* p. 51.

virtues. Listen to this really original moralist: "The word pride, in the language of Christian moralists, is held in suspicion; it is used to stigmatize precious qualities, and even virtues."* " There is a certain elevation of soul which is only obtained by a habit of disdain."† "Disdain almost always produces a delicate style.... Disdain is a delicate and delicious luxury which a man enjoys by himself: it is discreet, for it suffices to itself."‡ And in the blasphemous romance which it has pleased him to call *Vie de Jésus*, this man, who, according to the words of a famous orator, has found means to make praise of the most repulsive form of blasphemy,§ extols our Lord Jesus Christ for having "founded that great doctrine of transcendent disdain, the true doctrine of the liberty of souls, which alone gives peace."‖

Is not this intoxication? is not this truly delirium? To have descended to the lowest degree of intellectual abjection, and there, haughty in the midst of ruin, pity those who, as Plato says, have not so far corrupted their understanding? What can there be in the intellectual order below Materialism, and that state in which reason, wholly stripped and corrupted, no longer believes in truth, and can no longer discern between that which

---

* *Essais de Morale et de Critique*, p. 174.
† *Ib.* p. 209.   ‡ *Ib.* p. 188.
§ M. de Montalembert, *Deuxième Discours prononcé à l'Assemblée Générale des Catholiques, tenue à Malines du 18 au 22 Août*, 1863.
‖ *Vie de Jésus*, p. 117.

is and that which is not? This is M. Renan's position, as his last writings testify. This singular leader of the pretended critical school in France is perhaps the most remarkable type of those subtle but corrupted minds, numerous enough at the present time, who have no concern as to what is true or what is false, and who lull themselves with images and a vain sound of words. Nor is this class of mind new. It was dominant in Greece at the epoch when Socrates appeared. Protagoras and Gorgias are the real ancestors of M. Renan and our other contemporary sophists. It is the glory of Socrates that he delivered his country from these public poisoners. Who will deliver European society of their miserable descendants?

By the side of the Materialists, Pantheists, sceptics, sophists of every kind, there is among unbelievers a large class of men who seek to maintain the fundamental dogmas of natural religion and the essential principles of moral order: these are the spiritualistic rationalists. The supporters of spiritualistic Rationalism recognize the existence of a personal God, distinct from the world, infinitely perfect. With Christians, they affirm that this God is one, and the Creator of all things; they defend the spiritual nature, liberty, and immortality of the soul; they admit an absolute and immutable moral law, the necessary basis of the distinction between moral good and evil, and they confess that rewards and punishments are reserved in a future life for men who observe or violate the precepts of this law; but they do not define the nature of these rewards and punishments, nor their duration. They say, moreover, that man owes a worship to God ; but they do not say in what this worship consists. This, in its essential features, is the moral and religious creed of many cultivated and honest minds who will not receive the Christian Faith, and absolutely reject whatever is supernatural.

It is the fear of the supernatural which causes these Rationalists, without denying the doctrine of Divine Providence, singularly to lower it. They reject all positive intervention of God in the world, because otherwise they must admit miracles, which would destroy their system. They do not even recognize the legitimacy and efficacy of prayer in the sense of petition : they pretend that God can not derogate from the general law of the universe in order to bestow certain favors, whether in the moral, religious, on material order, on any individual man who asks for them.

What becomes of religion with such doctrines as these ? To what is the dogma of Providence reduced ? To this : that God exercises no direct action on the world ; that he is a stranger to the life of humanity ; that truth and error, good and evil, the happiness and misery of man, are matters of profound indifference to him ; that it is enough for him to have created the world ; henceforth he has no further concern with it, that it must go on as it can, and that each creature must suffice to itself. I protest that I cannot understand how any one who believes in a personal and infinitely perfect God can reduce him to act such a part as this. Truly this God of Rationalism is but the statue of God; he is not the living God. This is the remark of M. Guizot, who was long in the trammels of Rationalism: "The best among Rationalists," he says, "only suffer the statue of God (if such an expression may be used)—the statue only, an image, a piece of marble—to subsist in the world and in the human soul. God himself is no longer there. Christians alone possess the living God. It is this living God," adds the statesman, "whom we need. It is requisite for our present and future salvation that faith in the supernatural order, that reverence for and submission to the supernatural order, should be restored to the world and to the human soul in great minds as in simple minds, in the highest ranks as well as in the humblest. On this condition rests the truly efficacious and regenerating influence of religious belief. Without this it is superficial, and all but vain."*

Assuredly spiritualistic Rationalism—which is undoubtedly the best, the noblest, the most honest form of unbelief, is, in my opinion, anything but reasonable.

* *Méditations et Etudes morales,* preface. Paris, 1852.

PART II.

CHAPTER I.

What Faith is.

MANY people have a strange idea of religious Faith. Some look upon it as only an office of the imagination, or, at most, of the feelings. According to them, religion is wholly in the sensible part of the soul; reason has nothing to do with it. Hence they consider all religions as indifferent in themselves. Religious feeling may be produced under diverse forms; these forms are of no importance; it is sufficient that the feeling be sincere, and that it show itself by the homage of a respectful submission to the Divinity. The question of doctrine and truth wholly disappears; it is of no moment to know whether a religious belief be true or false, if it be conformable or contrary to reason; all is judged exclusively from the point of view of the heart. This is truly a senseless opinion, insulting alike to reason and to God. Yet a great number of men hold it, according to whom Christian Faith is a blind sentiment, more or less respectable, which may be good enough for the common people, but is unworthy of a cultivated mind guided by the light of reason.

On the other hand, men are to be found who place themselves at a wholly opposite point of view; who persuade themselves that faith is the work of the understanding alone, that feeling and the will have no part in it; and they conclude thence that faith is not free, that it in no way depends on us, and that if some receive the Christian creed whilst others reject it, it is because they see, or think they see, what is hidden from the others. If it were so, unbelief could never be a sin; at most, putting things at their worst, it would only be a mistake. Men who reason thus can have reflected but little on the part the will plays in the adhesion of the soul to truth.

Let us begin by recalling the principles of Catholic theology on the nature of faith. When these principles are known, it will be easier to discern the causes of infidelity. It is necessary to know exactly what the Christian Faith is, in order that we may comprehend what the obstacles are which hinder its birth and growth in a soul, that we may know what things are most likely to weaken or even extinguish it in a soul where it already exists.

To believe, in the religious and Christian sense of the word, is to adhere to any truth on the au-

The Principal Causes of Infidelity. 141

thority of God, who is the revealer of that truth. Human faith accepts a thing on the testimony of man ; Divine and Christian Faith on the testimony of God. We believe all the articles of the Catholic creed, because we are convinced that all these articles have been revealed by God, and consequently they have for their warrant the testimony of God himself. We do not adhere to such or such a doctrine as the object of our Faith, on the word of the Pope, or of the Church. In our eyes, the Church is but a means of going to God, a medium divinely established to communicate the teaching of God to us. The Church is not the Truth ; she is its guardian and its organ ; she bears witness to the Truth.

We must observe, by the way, that the Catholic Church and the Divine Revelation made in Jesus Christ are two things absolutely inseparable. From the moment we admit that God has made a divine and supernatural revelation to the human race, and that he has prescribed a religion for men to follow, we must also necessarily admit that his providence has established an authority charged to maintain this religion pure and entire, to preserve it, and to propagate it. It is absurd, supremely absurd, to suppose that God would reveal and establish the religion which men must follow in order to attain their end, and then leave this religion to itself, abandon it to chance, without any care for its fate, suffering it to become corrupt and to fade away by

contact with time, and the interested caprices and innumerable moral and intellectual weaknesses which human nature continually displays. A God who could act thus could not be to us a personal God, infinitely wise and perfect; he would be a being as inexplicable as the god of Epicurus, a god whom reason must disown. Many Protestant authors, in spite of their prejudices, recognize the necessary and indissoluble union between Christian revelation and the Church. "When we start from a supernatural principle in religion," says Staeudlin, "we must necessarily admit that the Divinity, who has deigned to make this revelation to man, must have taken care that it should not be abandoned to the arbitrary judgment of men; not to admit this principle is to argue inconsistently."*
"What the doctrine of Divine Providence is with regard to the creation," says another Protestant writer, "such is the doctrine of the infallibility of the Church with regard to Divine Revelation. They must stand or fall together."†

The Divine Word, which the Church does but repeat and explain to men, cannot deceive. God is Truth, and the Truth does not lie. When it is once thoroughly established that a doctrine comes from God, it would be absurd to demand other proofs of the truth of this doctrine. People do not ask Truth if it speaks the truth. Our Faith, resting on

---

* *Staeudlin's Magazin*, vol. iii. p. 83.
† *N. Quartalschrift*, Jahrgang ix. n. 3.

the authority of the Divine Word, is therefore sheltered from all error; the foundation on which it rests is immovable. It is supremely reasonable, for it depends on the veracity of God himself, who is infinite reason.

We are certain that the doctrines to which we adhere by Divine Catholic Faith really come from God. We do not admit lightly or without cause the fact of Divine Revelation; we believe it on the authority of truths whose evidence in our eyes is absolutely incontestable, and twenty times more striking than that which surrounds the best authenticated historical facts. These proofs form what is called in theology *motives of credibility*. These are the preliminaries of faith — preliminaries which human reason has a right to demand, and may examine by the light of earnest, upright, loyal criticism. Christianity does not fear an attentive and thorough examination of its title-deeds. On the contrary, it calls for it. But people must not deceive themselves. However evident the motives of credibility may be in themselves, they do not suffice to produce faith in the soul; they prepare the way for faith, but they do not create it. The causes on which faith depends are higher, and of a more interior nature. Here we must strive to understand thoroughly the teaching of Catholic theology, throwing light, as it does, upon depths whose existence is not even suspected by multitudes of inattentive and superficial minds.

St. Thomas Aquinas gives the following definition of faith: "To believe is an act of the understanding adhering to Divine Truth by command of the will, which is moved by the grace of God. The act of faith is subject to free will in relation with God, and therefore it is meritorious."* We shall make a brief commentary on this definition, in which all is comprised. Faith is the result of the combined action of God and man. Let us see first what man does; then we will show what he receives from God, and how far he must be aided by God in order to believe with a supernatural and true faith.†

The understanding does not act alone in man in the formation of the act of Faith, but the will also, and principally; it is the act of the whole soul, with all its faculties, all its powers. To believe is assuredly, as St. Thomas says, an act of the understanding, because the object of Faith is Divine Truth, and truth in itself is the object of the understanding, and not of the will; the understanding is made to know that which is true, the will to love and conform itself to that which is good. It is therefore exact to say that faith is the direct and immediate act of the understanding,

---

* "Ipsum credere est actus intellectus assentientis veritati divinæ ex imperio voluntatis a Deo motæ per gratiam; et sic subjacet libero arbitrio in ordine ad Deum; unde actus fidei est meritorius."—*Summa Theol.* 2, 2, q. ii. art. 9.

† "Credere immediate est actus intellectus, quia objectum hujus actus ost *verum*, quod proprie pertinet ad intellectum."—*Ibid.* q. iv. art. 3.

not of the will. But it is only by the intervention of the will which moves, directs, and commands it, that the understanding accepts Divine Truth, and gives adhesion and assent to it. There is no constraint upon the will with regard to the direction it shall take, and in which it will be followed by the understanding: the will is free. Undoubtedly it can, under grave responsibility, choose between two contrary directions, and, consequently, either unite and bind the understanding to truth, or turn it away, and precipitate it into error. On this account, the act of faith, on the firm adhesion of the understanding to Divine Truth, is meritorious; it is a free act, free with a liberty subject to trial, and not yet fixed in the love and possession of the truth.

Suarez justly observes that, to accomplish the act of faith, it is not sufficient that there be no repugnance in the will to believe; it is necessary that by a positive act it move the understanding to attach itself to revealed truth.* It is, then, the will that is the principal agent of faith in us. It is not the understanding, but the will, which decides with regard to faith. In order to believe, we must will to believe; will it positively and seriously; the direction and assent of the understanding depend upon the will. In this sense St. Augustine says, and St. Thomas repeats after him, that Faith

* *De Fide.* disp. vi. sect. vi. n. 7.

dwells in the will of those who believe: "Fides consistit in credentium voluntate."*

I fear that this doctrine, which gives so great a preponderance to the will in the act of faith, may astonish and disturb more than one of my readers, who are accustomed to look only to the understanding when the knowledge and acceptance of truth are in question. But they may be reassured. I am confident that if they will read to the end, they will see that the principles of Catholic theology, on the adhesion of the soul to Divine Truth, are in harmony with the fundamental and intimate laws of our nature, and can be misunderstood only by a prodigiously superficial psychology. I will confine myself, for the present, to some short remarks.

Most theologians, in explaining the free and meritorious character of the act of faith, content themselves with observing, "That the object of faith is obscure to us—not evident in itself. Thus the dogmas of the Holy Trinity, of the Incarnation, of the Redemption, of the Eucharist, for example, are certainly not in themselves evident to our reason; they are mysteries; that is to say, obscure truths superior to reason, truths in which," as Leibnitz remarks, "sober minds will always find sufficient explanation to believe, and never as much as is needed to comprehend." † The

---

* Ap. St. Thom. loc. cit. q. vi. a. 1.
† *Discours de la Conformité de la Foi avec la Raison*, n. 56.

proofs which bear testimony to the existence of Divine Revelation are evident—they ought to be evident, they are the motives of credibility—but the things revealed, being above reason, remain obscure; not wholly obscure, doubtless, for in that case they could not be known, and faith would be impossible, but in that kind of half-obscurity which excludes evidence. This defect of evidence, as theologians justly remark, explains the possibility of hesitation and denial on the part of the understanding, and shows the necessity of the preponderance given to the will in the accomplishment of the act of faith.

This is elementary to any one who reflects. The mind, not being subjugated by evidence, may accept or reject the truth that is offered to it; all depends on the disposition of the will.

But we must go further. Supposing the truths proposed were not superior to reason, a sad and daily experience shows that reason might still reject them. Liberty plays a considerable part even in the domain of truths of the natural order, on which the clearness of rational evidence sheds light. Is not the existence of God evident? And yet men are to be found—I mean learned men, men of cultivated minds—who are ignorant of God, or who form so unnatural a notion of him that the God whom they seem to acknowledge presents none of the features of the living and true God. What is more evident than the freedom and immortality of the soul? And yet these truths meet with contradiction, and obstinate contradiction. Whence comes this? Do not these facts offer abundant proof that the assent of the mind remains free even in the face of evidence? How could it be free if the will—the sole power in us which is free—did not intervene in the judgments we form?

We must not forget that our understanding is not a solitary faculty, living and acting by itself alone in entire independence. It is closely united to the other powers of our soul, and is moved and governed by the will, the centre and chief of these powers. The will makes the man in the moral and religious order, as it does in the social order; and it exercises an incalculable power even in the order which appears purely intellectual. I shall return to this subject hereafter.

Let us now show, according to Catholic teaching, what part is necessarily borne by God in the act of faith.

"To believe," says St. Thomas, "depends on the will of those who believe; but the will of man must be prepared by God through grace, and thus be raised to the supernatural order."* Faith appertains to the supernatural order; hence it cannot be the work of nature, nor of our soul abandoned to

---

* "Credere quidam in voluntate credentium consistit; sed oportet quod voluntas hominis præparetur a Deo per gratiam, ad hoc quod elevetur in ea quæ sunt supra naturam."—*Summa Theol.* 2, 2, q. vi. ad 3um.

its own strength. Let us hear the second Council of Orange on this point, whose decisions have been received as rules of faith throughout the whole Catholic Church. " If any one shall say that by the powers of nature we can do any good in order to the salvation of eternal life—that we can think or choose as we ought, or consent to the preaching of salvation, that is to say, to the Gospel, without the light and inspiration of the Holy Spirit, who gives to all the sweetness which makes us consent to and believe the truth—such an one is seduced by the spirit of heresy, and hears not the voice of God, which says in the Gospel, ' Without me you can do nothing.' (St. John xv. 5.)"* "If any one shall say that the beginning as well as the increase of faith, and even the pious sentiment by which we believe in him who justifies the ungodly, and attain the new birth of holy baptism, is in us naturally, and not by the gift of grace, that is to say, by the inspiration of the Holy Spirit, which corrects our will, and turns it from infidelity to faith, from impiety to piety—such an one shows himself opposed to the apostolical dogma, the blessed Paul saying, ' Being confident that he who hath begun a good work in you will perfect it unto the day of Christ Jesus,' (Phil. i. 6 ;) and elsewhere, ' Unto you it is given for Christ, not only to believe in him, but also to suffer for him' (v. 29 ;) and, ' For by

* Caput vii.

grace you are saved through faith, and that not of yourselves, for it is the gift of God.' (Ephes. ii. 8.)"*

These decisions of the Council of Orange were confirmed by Pope Boniface II. In the letter which the Pontiff wrote on this subject to the illustrious Saint Cesarius of Arles, who had presided over the Council, we read: "We rejoice greatly that in the Council which you and certain Bishops of Gaul have held, the Catholic Faith has been followed, in defining by common consent, as you point out, that the faith by which we believe in Jesus Christ is given us by Divine Grace preventing us. . . . For it is a certain and Catholic dogma, that in all good works, of which faith is the chief, even before we have yet willed, Divine Mercy prevents us, in order that we may will; it accompanies us when we will, and follows us in order that we may persevere in the faith."†

Grace must therefore prevent our will, and incline us to consent to, and to believe revealed truth; it must accompany and sustain our changeable and inconstant will in this holy disposition; finally, it must follow the good will it has inspired, and help us to will to adhere always to the Word of God.

Nothing in the principles of Christianity can be more simple or more logical than this doctrine. We are not created for a purely natural end, one to be realized by the mere exercise of our natural powers, but for a supernatural end, above the reach of

* Caput v. † Labbe, *Concil.* tom. iv. col. 1688.

our faculties. This end is to see God face to face, or in his essence, as he is in himself, a single nature subsisting in three distinct persons; to possess him fully, and to enjoy the happiness attached to such possession. This vision of God, this beatitude, is manifestly above nature. How can we attain it? The happiness of a free and intelligent being consists in the realization of his end, and he must achieve it by his own acts; but the acts of man, in themselves, are not means proportioned to an end superior to nature. In order, therefore, that there may be harmony or proportion between the means and the end, it is necessary that these acts should be elevated, ennobled, transformed, by a principle superior to nature, and thus become supernatural; this principle is grace. Is it not a common axiom that means must be proportioned to their end? If, then, the end of man is supernatural, his acts, which are the means by which he must attain this end, must of necessity be supernatural, and consequently animated by a principle superior to nature. This reasoning appears to me geometrically exact.

Grace, by which God enlightens our understanding with a supernatural light, attracts, fortifies, and elevates our will, sows in us the seed of that higher life which is to become the Christian life, and will be the initiation and first faint sketch of that eternal life, which begins upon earth and will be finished and consummated in the glory of heaven. "Grace and glory," says St. Thomas, "are generically one; because grace is nothing else than a certain beginning of glory in us."* Now faith is precisely the beginning of that supernatural life, of which the glory of the beatific vision will be but the marvellous completion. It is by faith that man enters of full right, if I may thus speak, in the supernatural order. It is, therefore, easy to understand the indispensable necessity of grace for the act of faith.

There are three kinds of life possible to man in this world: the life of the body or of the senses; the life of mere natural reason; the life of grace, raised above nature by faith, and working by charity. "The first," says a religious writer, whose simple, frank language I will venture to borrow, "is the life of an animal; the second, the life of a man; the third, the life of a Christian. . . . The carnal man," adds this author, "the man wholly immersed in the animal life—a drunkard, for example—can conceive nothing beyond eating and drinking, nothing beyond the body and what flatters the senses. All that is intellectual—science, poetry, moral beauty—all is folly to him. The rationalist or philosopher, wholly taken up with nature, can conceive nothing above human reason. All that is supernatural and divine—faith, grace—is folly to him. He is to the Christian, what the drunkard is to the philosopher. The carnal man

* Loc. cit. q. iv. art. 9 ad 2m.

may mistake or deny the intellectual order: that order, none the less, exists. In the same way the rationalist may mistake or deny the supernatural order, the order of grace: that order, none the less, exists. The carnal man, who would raise himself to the intellectual order, must in some sort die to himself, in order to enter a new state of existence, a new world. The rationalist who would raise himself to the supernatural order, the order of grace and faith, is obliged in some sort to die to himself, in order to enter a new state of existence, a new world such as he had never even suspected. The carnal man in becoming a rational man ceases not to be a man, but becomes better and nobler. The rational man in becoming a man of faith ceases not to become a rational man, he becomes a man of Divine reason."*

Rationalism recognizes only the first two of these states—life according to the senses and life according to reason; it altogether denies the supernatural life, the life of faith. Such a denial is precisely as well founded as that of the animal man, who denies the life of reason because it is extinct in him. Maine de Biran, after having himself traversed all the phases of Rationalism, came to discern clearly these three states of existence in man, by simple psychological observation; and with the exception of a few inaccuracies of

* Rohrbacher, *De la Grace et de la Nature*, xxxii. and xl.

language, unavoidable in one who is a stranger to theological study, he has described them well.

He names these three conditions of life, the animal life, the human life, the spiritual life.*

Whatever blind philosophy may say, faith does not destroy nor lower reason, but, on the contrary, strengthens and raises it in a singular degree. Did faith lower the reason of St. Augustine, St. Thomas, Leibnitz, Bossuet, of Joseph Görres? Faith gives to human reason a superior light, which, at the same time that it discovers absolutely new horizons to our gaze, illuminates the domain which the eyes of our understanding have already discerned, with a clearer and brighter light. Philosophers who reject faith to confine themselves to mere reason, are just like astronomers who would lay aside the telescope, to study the heavens with their naked eye. Faith is the telescope of human reason. Armed with this powerful help, our understanding has a clearer perception of that which is within its reach, and in the heaven of heavens, beyond its natural horizon, it discovers new and marvellous worlds, to which its unaided vision could never have attained. To reject faith is manifestly to diminish reason, and to deprive it of its most wonderful auxiliary to knowledge.

* See *Les Nouveaux Essais d'Anthropologie*, in the *Œuvres inédites* of Maine de Biran, published by Ernest Naville, voL iii. pp. 534, 535. Paris, 1859. The principal questions relating to grace, in the theological and philosophical points of view, have been fully treated in vol. iiL of *Dogmes Catholiques*.

The Principal Causes of Infidelity. 155

Faith, inasmuch as it is light, produces a twofold effect in us: first, it reveals to us truths of the supernatural order; next, it adds to the rational evidence of the light of reason in the circle of truths of the purely natural order, such as the existence of God, his attributes, the Creation of the world, Providence, the spiritual nature, liberty, and immortality of the soul. More than this, faith, as light and as power, purifies the eye of the understanding from a thousand foreign elements, which embarrass it, and hinder its free exercise; it gives a movement to the will which turns it toward God and the intelligible world, and at the same time raises the whole soul, helps it to shake off the yoke of those things that are inferior to its nature, and leads it toward those higher regions in which its destiny calls it to move and live. Faith is a power which struggles against the inclination, unhappily innate in fallen man, which drags our soul toward inferior objects, and imparts to us a contrary inclination. Plato would say that faith restores to the human soul the wings that were broken in its fall.

Let no one infer from the Catholic dogma that grace is necessary to enable us to believe with a divine supernatural faith, that there are therefore men necessarily condemned to be without faith, because God has not given them the grace to believe. The Church — which knows God, and beholds in him a compassionate Father, and not an unjust master, gathering where he has not sown—teaches that he refuses grace to none. It is also a Catholic dogma that God wills all men to be saved, and that he offers to all the grace necessary to enable them to acquire the ineffable glory to which he bids them. The Council of Trent declares that "God commands nothing impossible; when he orders anything, he at the same time warns us to do what we can, to ask for what we cannot do of ourselves, and he will help us to do it."*

To ask for what we are unable to attain of ourselves is the ordinary condition which God imposes for the bestowing of his favors. He wills that we, who are created and essentially dependent beings, should confess our own insufficiency, and implore the aid of him from whom light and strength descend. The old man who discovered the teaching of the Gospel to the philosopher Justin, when he was seeking for the truth, said to him, " Pray that the gates of light may be opened before you; for no one can see and comprehend these things unless God and his Christ give him understanding."† Justin followed this counsel, and was rewarded by a faith which he sealed with his blood. If men who do not believe would pray as this ardent and generous philosopher prayed, they would, I am convinced, soon believe with a faith as firm as his.

* Sess. vi. cap. xi.
* *Dial. cum Tryph.* n. 7. See above, p. 37.

CHAPTER II.

Infidelity—In what it consists.

INFIDELITY is the opposite of faith. What we have just said of the nature and conditions of faith may make us understand what constitutes the ground of unbelief. But we will add a few words to describe it in a more precise and complete manner.

Generally speaking, we call any one an infidel or unbeliever who does not bend his reason before Divine Revelation and submit to its authority. Infidelity is the denial of all Divine Revelation—of the primitive revelation made to the father of the human race, continued later to the patriarchs, then to the prophets of God's people, and finally accomplished in Jesus Christ, the Author and Finisher of our Faith. Unbelief denies the supernatural order of which we spoke just now, and the miraculous order which supposes and involves a Divine Revelation. It denies any determinate and positive intervention of God in the history of humanity. It absolutely ignores the immense divine fact which occupies the two epochs of history—the epoch of the ages anterior to Jesus Christ, and the epoch of the ages which followed him—the fact which shines with incomparable brilliancy in Christian society, the most moral, learned, civilized, powerful society that the world has ever seen. The infidel pretends to rely solely upon reason; he admits no other light than the natural light; he recognizes no other facts than those which can be explained by natural causes; miracles in his eyes are a chimera as much as Divine Revelation; he rejects all that surpasses the power of nature, as well as all that exceeds the light of reason.

Such is the general character of infidelity as it shows and asserts itself in the midst of Christian Europe. All our unbelievers, to whatever school they belong, and however great may be their differences, agree in the denial of the supernatural and the miraculous; all make a boast of recognizing only reason and nature. Therefore the names of Naturalism and Rationalism express exactly the common principle which unites them.

St. Thomas teaches that infidelity, like faith, is an act of the understanding, but an act commanded by the will. He says, "Infidelity, as well as faith, is in the understanding as in its immediate subject; but it is in the will as in its first mover."* He adds: "It is the contempt of the will which causes the dissent of the understanding, and it is in this dissent that infidelity essentially consists.

* " Infidelitas, sicut et fides, est quidem in intellectu sicut in proximo subjecto; in voluntate autem sicut in primo motivo."—Loc. cit. q. x. art. 2.

Hence the cause of infidelity is in the will, although infidelity itself is in the understanding.* Infidelity having its cause in the will, is, like faith, a free act; it is the fruit of a free decision of the mind. Therefore it is imputable. Faith is a virtue, and infidelity is a vice."†

It is scarcely necessary to observe, that it does not follow from hence that every man who does not believe in the Christian Revelation is necessarily guilty. A man may be unbelieving and yet not an infidel in the strict sense of the word. Infidelity, properly so called, as St. Thomas defines it, supposes that the ignorance of Divine Revelation is not wholly involuntary. There are men who do not know, and who, morally speaking, cannot know, Jesus Christ; therefore these men do not believe in him: but their infidelity is a purely negative infidelity, as St. Thomas calls it; they are *non-believers* rather than infidels; this absence of faith is not imputable to them because it is nowise in their will. There is no real, and consequently no culpable infidelity, in the theological sense of the word, except voluntary infidelity. *Where there is no freedom there is no sin*, is an elementary principle of morals. But there is another principle no less elementary which is too often

---

* "Dicendum quod contemptus voluntatis causat dissensum intellectus, in quo perficitur ratio infidelitatis: *unde causa infidelitatis est in voluntate; sed ipsa infidelitas est in intellectu.*"—Loc. cit. q. x. art. 2 ad 2 m.
† St. Thomas, *ibid.* art. 1.

forgotten, and it is this: a thing may be voluntary directly or indirectly, in itself or in the cause upon which it depends. God alone knows the secret dispositions of the soul, and the obstacles which many unbelievers oppose, more or less voluntarily, to faith. It is indisputable that the will plays an important part in infidelity, and this will be better understood as we proceed.

The diverse forms of Rationalism, which are but different degrees of infidelity, would suffice to justify the doctrine of St. Thomas on the first and fundamental cause of unbelief, as I have already remarked in speaking of faith. All unbelievers affirm, with marvellous unanimity, that they will obey reason and reason alone; they add, with one voice, that the language of reason is sufficiently clear on all questions which affect the destiny of man, and that they need no other teacher. If it be thus, whence arise those radical differences which divide the faithful and respectful disciples of reason into two opposite camps? Whence comes it that Renan, an atheist and materialist, contradicts, on all the principles of morality, Jules Simon, who, like him, recognizes no other authority than reason? Is it not because all do not equally listen to the voice of reason, whose sovereignty they proclaim in theory whilst they ignore and resist it in fact? How many men assume toward reason the same attitude which the best of the rationalists assume toward faith! The sophists, by an evil and culpable disposition of the will, ignore the authority of reason, as the rationalists ignore the authority of faith.

There are rebels and revolutionists in the kingdom of reason as there are in the kingdom of faith. There are also, which is sometimes more excusable, sick and languishing minds whom the light wounds, and who see things only through a deceptive medium. This intellectual malady has too often a voluntary cause; but sometimes it is the result of education and circumstances from which its victims have been unable to free themselves.

I have already pointed out the principal forms of contemporary infidelity. In the first half of this century, Pantheism reckoned the greatest number of celebrated followers; now materialism is regaining favor, and is received and supported by many learned unbelievers. Evidently neither pantheists nor materialists follow the natural light of reason; they are in open revolt against it, declared rebels to its authority. Spiritualistic Rationalism looks upon them in this light as we do. There are also among our infidels sceptics who no longer believe in any certainty, and who, despairing to find truth, close their eyes and bury themselves in a factitious slumber which completes the ruin of their understanding. They are sick, and imagine they will find health and rest in suicide. Spiritualistic Rationalism is certainly the most reasonable form of infidelity; but its most distinguished representatives act with regard to the motives of credibility of the Christian Faith—which are as evident as the freedom and immortality of the soul—in the same way that sceptics, materialists, and pantheists act with regard to the evident truths of reason. I am aware of the fine pretexts with which they cloak their unbelief; but are not they themselves also aware of the pretexts with which the miserable crowd of sophists cover their daring negations? Let them lay aside pretexts, let them go to the bottom of things, and with their hand on their conscience, dare to ask themselves seriously and sincerely why they do not believe.

CHAPTER III.

It is impossible to attribute the Infidelity of the Present Day to the Progress of Reason and Science— Numerous Conversions among Learned Men— Augustin Thierry and Maine de Biran.

EFORE pointing out in detail the real causes of unbelief, we will again glance at the pretext ordinarily employed by men of all kinds who reject the Christian Faith. All, whether sceptics, atheists, pantheists, or spiritualistic rationalists, pretend that our belief, which was perhaps good for unenlightened ages, cannot sustain critical inquiry in the actual condition of the human mind; reason goes beyond it; science exposes its failings and errors. Certainly it is strange to see a religion which has been at the head of civilization for eighteen centuries, and whose creed has been accepted, defended, glorified by the most eminent intellects and most illustrious philosophers, from St. Justin to Lacordaire and Joseph Görres, condemned with such self-sufficiency, and, we may add, with such levity. Will any one dare to say that there has ever been a society equal to the Christian society for power of reasoning and extent of knowledge? For the

rest, it seems to me that the historical portion of this work has completely disposed of the fine pretext put forward by rationalists of every shade. I protest that I can with difficulty regard the proud anti-Christian declarations of contemporary unbelief in a serious light, and were it not that charity for human souls obliges me to bear with the most unreasonable prejudices, I should be tempted to answer them only by contemptuous silence. But it is the duty of the disciples and ministers of Jesus Christ to compassionate all the intellectual and moral infirmities of their brethren.

It is unnecessary here to examine and discuss directly the motives of the non-acceptance which Rationalism opposes, in the name of philosophy and science, to the teaching of the Christian Faith; this has been done elsewhere.* We will only recall a few contemporary facts, which, in our opinion, demonstrate that infidelity has nothing in common with scientific progress.

In the early ages of Christianity, pagan philosophers ridiculed the simplicity of Christians, and represented them as the enemies of reason, philosophy, and science. Celsus and Porphyry, not to mention other names, attacked the Gospel upon principles similar to those which Rationalism now employs. But these attacks did not hinder philosophers and learned men of the first order, such as St. Justin, Athenagoras, Tertullian, Clement of

---

* *Les Dogmes Catholiques*, etc.

The Principal Causes of Infidelity. 165

Alexandria, Arnobius, and St. Augustine, from bowing their reason before the authority of the Gospel, and submitting their understandings to the Christian Faith. Who, in these days, speaks of the criticisms of Celsus or Porphyry? And since a new paganism has sought to raise its head in Europe, the same phenomenon is reproduced before our eyes. Whilst a certain number of men denounce the Christian Faith as the antithesis of philosophy and science, men of eminent minds are to be met with, who, after having passed the greater part of their lives in infidelity, return to this Faith, and proclaim that all the objections of Rationalism, which had so long held them back, have no pretensions to science, and rest upon prejudices unworthy of an earnest mind. This is a fact of the highest importance, which would alone suffice to show the puerility of infidel pretensions. Since the beginning of this century, how many learned men have been seen to desert the standard of Rationalism and range themselves under the banner of the Faith! Nor can it be said of these learned converts, as it is said of us, that in their profession of the Faith they do but obey the prejudices of education; for on entering the Church they have been obliged to break with their past life, and often with habits of mind contracted since the first real dawn of reason. Who will dare to say that men like Frederick Schlegel, Maine de Biran, Lherminier, Augustin Thierry, with many more as learned as they, were strangers to the progress of modern criticism, or deficient in intellectual independence?

We will pause only at two names, Augustin Thierry and Maine de Biran, of whom one represents historical, and the other philosophical criticism.

Augustin Thierry claims a place in the first ranks of the restorers of historical research in France. No one, in the annals of literature, presents a more wonderful example of perseverance in labor and devotion to science. "For thirty years," says a priest, the friend and confident of the illustrious historian, "it was the will of God to shroud this luminous understanding in material darkness, and imprison this energetic will in a motionless body. But the soul confined in this prison, and wearing this chain, continued its work and its persevering search after God and his truth. . . . Perfectly blind, entirely paralyzed, instead of giving way to heaviness and dulness, he watched, meditated, listened, and dictated; and with what brilliancy, what enthusiasm! His life was regulated and disciplined by the inflexible exactness of an almost religious rule."* This energetic and unconquerable mind entered on the study of history with the most hostile prepossessions against the Christian Faith, and he often evinced

---

* Lettre à Mgr. l'Archevêque de Paris sur les derniers instants de M. Augustin Thierry par le Père Gratry, dans *Le Correspondant*, 25 Juin, 1856.

great injustice toward the Church. But what was the result of his researches and meditations? It was the profound conviction that all the philosophical and historical difficulties of which unbelief makes so much, are but phantoms which fade away as soon as they are exposed to the light of serious examination. Let us hear Father Gratry:

"Having abandoned infidelity, as he himself has often told me, he soon learnt from the sincere study of men and of history that infidelity does not explain the mystery of the world, and that the living power which leads mankind is religion. History further showed him that this religion can be no other than Christianity. But as his mind rose by degrees from error to truth, he thought at first to have found the pure doctrine of the Gospel in Protestantism. At that time, he sought for light at Geneva.

"Then (these are his own words) I had no notion of the history of the Church. When I had cast my eyes over it, I saw clearly that Protestantism could not be the religion founded by Jesus Christ. Protestantism and history are wholly incompatible. The Protestant system has been forced to construct a fictitious history for its own use. I am astonished that people can still maintain themselves on such ground. How is it that they do not see that Catholicism is found entire in the first four centuries?" Another day, quite recently, he said to one of the Fathers of the Oratory, M. Pinaud: "People sometimes maintain—and it is a prejudice I shared for a long time—that the doctrine of the Church is formed of pieces and fragments. How false this is! What admirable unity we find in her teaching! The examination of the text soon overthrows this error."*

In the rationalist world, in the midst of which Augustin Thierry had passed his life, people wondered that so many learned men should be converted to Catholicism, and submit the reason they had so long held in independence to the authority of the Church. A week before his death this learned and conscientious man spoke of this fact to Father Gratry: "Many persons cannot understand how it happens, or whence it comes, that so many should return to the Catholic Church in spite of objections and difficulties. It is very simple: it is because Catholicism is the Truth. It is the true religion of mankind. Pretended philosophical objections are not philosophical; on the contrary, all the philosophy of all times and all places is found in the Catholic Doctrine. All truth centres in it, and men plunge into falsehood in proportion as they wander from it. This is why Lutheranism is worth less than Anglicanism, Calvinism less than Lutheranism, Unitarianism less than Calvinism, and so of the rest. On the other hand, I see no good reason against the Catholic Reli-

* Lettre à Mgr. l'Archevêque de Paris sur les derniers instants de M. Augustin Thierry par le Père Gratry, dans *Le Correspondant*, 25 Juin, 1856.

gion. If we consider the precepts of the Church, they are good, reasonable, salutary, even to the smallest practice: none can be omitted without leaving cause for regret. People do wrong to hesitate. They must come thither at last. True philosophy, true practical wisdom will be sure to lead men thither."*

Many false judgments, many religious errors, are to be found in the works of Augustin Thierry. He had intended to correct all that he had written against the Truth. Death surprised him in the midst of these generous labors. He said to Father Gratry: "I wish to correct all that I may have written, although in good faith, against the Truth, any wise. Every day and every night I implore God to give me time to finish this work, for it seems to me that in this I am working for God. I am often sustained and encouraged in my weariness and sleeplessness by this thought: I am God's workman. But do not repeat this," said he, with delicate modesty, " it would be presumptuous. I only say it to you."

"If I am not deceived," says Father Gratry in conclusion, " this example will become historical; it will be salutary to many; it will raise many from despair; it will cure the blindness of many."* Cer-

---

* Lettre à Mgr. l'Archevêque de Paris sur les derniers instants de M. Augustin Thierry par le Père Gratry, dans *Le Correspondant*, 25 Juin, 1856.
† *Ibid.*

tainly it is well calculated to dispel prejudices, an[d] to raise up weak and wavering minds.

The conversion of Maine de Biran is not les[s] striking than that of Augustin Thierry. Cousin sai[d] of this philosopher that he was "the greatest met[a]physician who had adorned France since Male[-] branche." We must not exaggerate: Maine de Bi[r]an is not a great metaphysician; he does not com[e] near Malebranche; but he is an eminent psycho[l]ogist, and undoubtedly one of the most sagaciou[s] and profound observers known to the philosoph[y] of the present century. How could a man becom[e] a metaphysician who had Condillac for his maste[r] and who has not studied in the school of Plato an[d] St. Augustine? Maine de Biran, like all his unbe[-]lieving contemporaries, began with the philosoph[y] of sensation and the degradation of materialism[.] How long a road he had to travel before he coul[d] reach the heights of Christian Faith! He di[d] travel this road, slowly, painfully; and by force o[f] perseverance and courage, he triumphed over th[e] obstacles of every kind which he met with on thi[s] long journey.

The serious observation of the phenomena o[f] thought and the activity of the *ego*, soon showe[d] Biran how empty was the philosophy of sensation[.] Materialism was vanquished, but the philosophe[r] did not dream of replacing it by Christianity. H[e] remained an infidel for a long time. The moralit[y] of stoicism pleased his noble and generous soul[.]

and he would have declared himself the disciple of Zeno had not the feeling of reality, always so vivid in him, shown him the chimerical side of this proud philosophy. His ideas with regard to the nature of religion were most false. He wrote thus in 1815: "Religion is a sentiment of the soul, rather than a belief of the mind; belief is subordinate to feeling."* This is exactly the inverse of the truth. At the same period he gave an account of the state of his soul and of the intellectual freedom with which he pursued the search after truth. "In my youth, and when I was prepossessed in favor of the materialistic systems which had seduced my imagination, I put aside all ideas which did not tend to this end. I was frivolous rather than insincere. But since my own ideas have led me far from these systems, I have had no prepossession in favor of any fixed conclusion at which I would arrive, no prepossession either in favor of belief or of unbelief. If I find God and the true laws of the moral order, it will be by good fortune, and I shall be more worthy of credit than they who, with so many prejudices, tend only to establish them by their theory."† Alas! this mind, which believed itself so free, obeyed unwittingly a multitude of prejudices fostered by anti-Christian ignorance.

Three years later, this philosopher, till then so

---

* *Journal Intime de Maine Biran*, p. 165. This work, edited by M. E. Naville, is, in truth, the history of the inward life of M. de Biran.
† *Ibid.* p. 179.

proud of his reason and moral strength, experienced an invincible need of leaning on God. "I leant on myself, I reckoned on my faculties, I hoped that they would continually develop, I expected great progress from time and labor; experience teaches me that I leant upon a feeble reed, agitated by the winds, broken by the tempest. Our faculties change and deceive our expectations; we have as little ground to believe in their power and duration as in their authority. 'When a man seeks not God, he doth himself more harm than the whole world and all his enemies can do him.'"*

This last sentence is taken from the *Following of Christ.* At the time when Biran wrote these lines, he was continually reading that incomparable book. The *Pensées de Pascal* and Fénélon's *Œuvres Spirituelles* were of the number of his favorite works. He tells us that in 1815 he was in the habit of beginning each day by reading a chapter of Holy Scripture.† This acquaintance with the doctrines revealed by God completed and corrected that work in his soul which his own moral and psychological experience had begun. As it happens almost always with earnest rationalists, this man, formerly so proud, so confident in his powers of reason and will, came scarcely to believe either in one or other; he had fallen into a kind of moral and intellectual depression. Men begin with

---

* *Journal Intime*, pp. 266, 277.
† See *Life of Maine de Biran* at the beginning of the *Journal Intime*," p. 91.

senseless pride, and end with despair, because they obstinately reject all support but self, that poor, feeble reed which bends and breaks so easily. But in this sad state of weakness, Biran happily turned toward God, and asked for light and strength from him who is the Truth and the Life. He prayed. When a soul prays, it is saved. We cannot too often repeat what reason and history agree in attesting, that prayer is the key of Faith. When a man humbly confesses his own insufficiency, and sincerely asks God to enlighten and strengthen him, he is very near believing and being a Christian.

Listen to Maine de Biran, to whom, a little while back, religion was but a matter of feeling, and Christian mysteries but dreams and chimeras: "Religious and moral belief, which reason does not originate, but which forms a basis and necessary starting-point of departure for reason, is now my sole refuge; and I find true science precisely there, where formerly, with the philosophers, I saw only dreams and chimeras."* "Religion alone solves the problems proposed by philosophy."†

"'The help of God," adds this undeceived rationalist, "is necessary for us even in those things which are, or appear to be, in our own power. I find myself stripped of all my faculties precisely because I relied too much on myself, and had not acquired the habit of confiding in the assistance of a

---

* *Journal Intime*, from May 26th to June 6th, 1815, pp. 267, 268.
† *Ibid.* June 30th.

superior power and asking for it by prayer, in order that I might be strengthened."*

" There are three very different kinds of disposition of the mind and soul: the first, which is that of most men, consists in living exclusively in the world of phenomena, (that is to say, the world of business, pleasure, glory,) and taking them for realities. Hence arise inconstancy, disgust, perpetual change. The second is that of reflective minds who long seek for truth in themselves and in nature by separating appearances from realities, and who, finding no fixed basis for this truth, in despair fall into scepticism. Finally, the third is that of souls enlightened by the light of Religion which alone is true and immutable. They alone have found a sure support; they are strong because they believe.†

. . . The greatest benefit Religion has bestowed upon us is the saving us from doubt and uncertainty, which are the greatest torment of the human mind, the true poison of life. In a mind destitute of religious belief all is undetermined, fugitive, and changeable."‡

The human mind is not made to walk alone; it walks securely only when leaning on Divine authority. It hesitates and totters even in the domain where it is naturally intended to move, unless sustained by the hand of God. This fact of daily experience Maine de Biran had observed in himself,

---

* *Journal Intime*, pp. 291, 292.
† *Ibid.* pp. 328, 329.   ‡ *Ibid.* p. 333.

The Principal Causes of Infidelity. 175

and in the society in which he lived. We rarely meet with infidels, even among the best, who firmly and constantly adhere to the truths of natural religion.

In the state of degradation and forfeiture in which man is born, he has need of the grace of God for two ends. First, he has need of a medicinal grace to cure the wounds of his nature, and to fortify his understanding and his will, so as to enable them, as Fénélon says, to attain the end of themselves, (*aller au bout d'elles-mêmes.*)* Maine de Biran saw perfectly the necessity of this grace; perhaps, as usually happens with minds that have relied too much on themselves and have been cruelly deceived, he exaggerated the extent of this necessity. Secondly, man has need of grace to raise himself to the supernatural order, which is, properly, the order of Faith, as we have already explained. Even before he fully embraced the Faith, our philosopher had clearly perceived the reality of this supernatural order, and the necessity of grace to attain it and maintain himself in it. No psychologist has ever more clearly seen, what Rationalism obstinately denies, that man is called to live a life superior to the life of the senses and of mere reason; that our nature, such as God has made it, calls for this life, but that it is not possible without supernatural help, which is grace. Let us hear

---

* This expression, rather trivial in its form, may be rendered: "To go as far as they are capable of going of themselves."

this scrupulous and profound observer of the human soul:

"There are not only two opposing principles in man, there are three; for there are three kinds of life and three orders of faculties. If there were perfect accordance and harmony between the sensitive and active faculties which constitute man, there would still be a superior nature—a third life—which would not be satisfied, and which would make us feel that there is another happiness, another wisdom, another perfection beyond the greatest human happiness, the highest wisdom and intellectual and moral perfection of which a human being is susceptible."* In the last pages of his *Journal Intime*, Biran returns continually to these three kinds of life: the life of the senses, the life of pure reason, the super-rational life or the life of faith; he has made the distinction between these three kinds of life one basis of his *Nouveaux Essais d'Anthropologie*. This superior life is instilled into us by the Spirit of God, which acts in us and communicates with our soul without being confounded with it.

"The delusion of philosophy is to consider the principle of spiritual life as exclusively belonging to the *ego*, and, because our *ego* can to a certain point free itself from dependence on sensible objects, to look upon it as independent of that other superior influence, whence it receives all that light which it does not originate. . . . I was formerly

* *Journal Intime*, p. 399.

puzzled to understand how the Spirit of Truth could be in us without being ourselves, without identifying itself with our own spirit, our *ego*. Now I comprehend the interior communication of a Spirit superior to us, which speaks to us, which we hear within us, which vivifies and fertilizes our spirit without being confounded with it. . . . This communication of the Spirit with our spirit—when we know how to call him to us, or to prepare for him a fit dwelling within us—is not only of faith, it is a veritable psychological fact.

"The whole doctrine of Christianity is comprised in love. When we have felt within ourselves the vivifying influence of the Divine Spirit, it is natural that we should love him, that we should invoke him without ceasing, as the food, support, principle of our life; that we should love him more than ourselves, for from him we hold an existence superior to that of self, and it is by love alone that we unite ourselves to the Spirit."* Rationalism denies this action of the Spirit of God in us, and the life which that action inspires and nourishes; but this denial, contradicted moreover by the principles of true philosophy, cannot prevail against a fact which all Christians experience, any more than the denial of a blind man would prevail against the fact that there is light, which all see whose eyes are open. "It is impossible," again says Maine de Biran, "to deny to the true believer

* *Journal Intime*, pp. 405, 410, 411.

who experiences in himself what he calls the effects of grace; who finds the repose and peace of his soul in the intervention of certain ideas or intellectual acts of faith, hope, and love; and who is thence able to satisfy his mind with regard to problems which no other system can solve; it is impossible, I say, to dispute what he experiences, and consequently not to recognize the true foundation there is in him, or in his religious belief, for those conditions of soul which constitute his consolation and his happiness."*

The following lines are the last which occur in the *Journal Intime* of Maine de Biran, and they deserve the attention of all men who think themselves strong enough to walk alone, and who proudly repulse the hand which God offers them by his Son Jesus Christ: " There should always be two, and we may say of man, even the individual man, *væ soli!* If a man is carried away by the unruly affections which absorb him, he can form no just judgment either of outward objects or of himself; if he abandon himself to them, he is unhappy and degraded, *væ soli!* A man may be ever so strong in reasoning powers and in human wisdom, but unless he feel himself sustained by a power and reason higher than himself, he will be unhappy; he may impose on others, he cannot impose on himself. True strength, true wisdom consists in walking in the presence of God, and in feeling his supporting

* *Journal Intime*, p. 405.

hand, otherwise *væ soli!* The stoic is either alone, or with the belief in his own strength, which deceives him; the Christian walks in the presence of God and with God, by the Mediator whom he has taken for the guide and companion of his present and future life."

These lines, the truth of which every sincere and upright mind will attest, were penned by Maine de Biran on the 17th May, 1824. Two months later he died, with sentiments of lively faith, consoled and fortified by the presence of our Divine Mediator, who came to visit him in the Sacrament of his love.

Let superficial and vain minds, who so presumtuously take their stand on the progress of reason, then see whither it led one of the deepest thinkers of this age.

In the face of such examples, how can the absurd prejudice be explained which maintains that Christian Faith is incompatible with the progress of reason and science? We have seen, and still see at this moment, learned men, men of the highest intellect, the most illustrious *savants* of France, Germany, England, and America, return to the Faith which never grows old, and, after having scrutinized all, tried all, proclaim that this Faith is the torch of science, the infallible guide of true progress; and are not those who have always kept the faith of their baptism as strong in reasoning, as well informed in the progress of science, as the unbelievers amongst whom they live? Let men cease to justify their infidelity by seeking refuge in a pretended incompatibility between Catholic Faith and modern science. Such an excuse is unworthy of a sincere mind. The real causes of infidelity are not to be found in the progress of information. We will now endeavor to show what they are.

CHAPTER IV.

Real Causes of Infidelity—First Cause, Ignorance of Religion.

FAITH, as we have seen, is an act of the understanding, but an act prescribed by the will—a free act. The cause of unbelief may be in the understanding or in the will, or in both these faculties combined; that is to say, in the whole soul. We will begin, then, with the understanding: we will seek to discover how and in what degree the understanding acts upon the influence of the will; this will lead us to study the state of the will, and with that, the state of the whole soul in infidels.

The first, and most common cause of infidelity, is ignorance of those truths which are the objects of faith. People know nothing of religion; they do not know what the Catholic Church—which keeps the Faith and prolongs the presence of Jesus Christ upon this earth—believes and teaches. In most cases, such ignorance is not wholly unprecedented. In the early ages of Christianity, many pagans, and among them many of the intellectual men of the time, reproached the disciples of the Incarnate Word with adoring the head of an ass!

Is it possible that after eighteen hundred years of Christian civilization, in a society born and nourished in the lap of the Church, men are still to be met with who heap upon us reproaches equally senseless? We see beside us learned men; men who have conscientiously studied the religions of Greece, of ancient Rome, of Persia, India, Egypt, and who yet speak of the religion of Jesus Christ, of the religion which has civilized Europe and is the light of the world, as a man born blind might speak of colors. Surely this phenomenon, which we daily witness, is one of the most alarming mysteries of the moral world.

Religious ignorance, as a cause of infidelity, shows itself in various degrees. There is total ignorance, and there is partial ignorance. But the greater number of unbelievers are totally ignorant of the Christian Religion, and have scarcely a vague notion of religion in general. We have seen that at the time when the soul of Maine de Biran began seriously to turn toward God, he looked upon religion as a matter of feeling in which reason had no part. Before that time, the thoughts of the philosopher had never even glanced at the religious order; to him that order had no existence. As long as Augustin Thierry was an infidel he studied history without any regard to religion—the only thing which can explain the history of the world. And when his eyes began to open—when he had a glimpse of the part assigned to religion, and thought he saw that religion could only be Christianity, he did not even then suspect that religious truth might be found in the Catholic Church. He knew nothing of the Church, or only knew her through the caricatures of her enemies. This man, who was so eager for knowledge, so curious in research, had never read with sincere attention a history of the Church, nor a complete and exact exposition of Catholic Doctrine. How can men believe, when they know nothing of what they ought to believe?

M. Droz, a member of the French Academy, admits that he became an infidel, not in consequence of a serious examination of Christian Truth, but without any examination; and because he was ill-informed with regard to the principles and doctrines of the Christian Religion, ignorantly and unreservedly accepting all the opinions of infidelity. This was an unhappy age, in which many marvellously gifted youths became, in some sort, the necessary prey of irreligion as soon as they entered the world: many, alas! receiving their first lessons of infidelity at the domestic hearth. Droz had received a Christian education; he had gone through his Humanities and course of philosophy in a college where the doctrines and practices of Christianity were held in honor. Still he was almost wholly ignorant of religion, and the first assaults of infidelity destroyed his belief. He did not, however, sink to the depth of moral and religious degradation as so many others had done; his noble mind, whilst it rejected Christian Revelation, preserved its belief in God, in the immortality of the soul, and in the moral law; he was one of the most upright and accomplished types of spiritualistic Rationalism. Let us listen to his confession; it will teach us how it happened that so many young men, at the beginning of this century, became infidels, and how it happens, doubtless, that so many become infidels at this day:

"I was almost always inattentive to religious instruction, and was far from having given those solid foundations to my belief which the times in which we were living required. The philosophy of the eighteenth century was predominant. Deists, in order to exercise influence, had no need either of profound learning or close logic; irreligion was the fashion—infidelity and indifference seemed to be in the air we breathed. Whilst I was occupying myself with literature, and prudently descending from poetry to prose, I constantly heard so many voices repeat with full conviction, 'The cause of Christianity has been judged and is lost for ever,' that I never doubted that I must start from this opinion as from a certain fact, when I would treat of religion with the enlightened men of the time. Thus did the youth of that time decide. God," adds this excellent man, "might have punished me for my infidelity more severely than he has done; he might have suffered me to fall into the degradation of the sophists, who seek in their pitiful pride to maintain that God does not exist, that man acts under the dominion of fate, and that morality is but a fable invented by ingenious men to dupe the weak and foolish. I was spared this excess of degradation; God, whose goodness surpasses our sins; God, to whom I owe so many acts of thanksgiving; God has never wholly abandoned me."*

Is it credible that this upright rationalist who was absorbed in the study of moral philosophy, and who read assiduously the essays of Montaigne, the *Tusculan Disputations* and *De Officiis* of Cicero, the *Dream of Scipio*, *Plutarch*, that he should never have dreamt of reading the Gospel, nor any of the great Christian moralists who have drawn freely from that incomparable source? In his eyes Christianity was irrevocably condemned, and all Christian literature was suppressed by the same blow. In this way did he understand and apply free examination.

I cannot forbear quoting one more page from the instructive *Aveux* of this once infidel moralist. "I did not lose time in seeking for arguments against Christianity; what was the use of doing so? Others had taken this trouble, and as far as I was concerned, the question was settled. In all my projects, that which occupied me most was the

* *Aveux d'un Philosophe Chrétien*, by Joseph Droz, of the French Academy, and of the Academy of Moral and Political Science, pp. 13-15.

desire to succeed in self-improvement. In spite of my love of literature and philosophy—far from paying a fanatical homage to Voltaire, the patriarch of irreligion, I was disgusted by his cynicism —I was grieved to behold an illustrious poet disgrace his genius by a parody of the history of the angelic heroine of France .... The so-called *Philosophy of History* excited still more painful feelings. In this libel against humanity, man is represented as a mass of vice, which renders him at once hateful and contemptible: what can be done with such a being? I loved liberty; I demanded it for all nations capable of understanding it; and when I saw the enthusiastic admirers of Voltaire proclaim themselves the champions of public liberty, the incoherency of their ideas confounded me. If man is made up of the tiger and the monkey, why should we speak of giving him liberty? On the contrary, bring a muzzle and chains; defend the world from the crimes of such a monster." *

We perceive that Droz, although an infidel, was not a follower of Voltaire. He was not a fanatic in his irreligion; he was an upright, moderate rationalist, striving to judge of men and things by the light of calm serene reason. But he knew very little of the Christian Religion, and unwittingly condemned it on the word of those disciples of Vol-

* *Aveux d'un Philosophe Chrétien*, pp. 17, 18.

taire whom he held in such slight estimation. Question those learned and distinguished men who in our own days have passed from Rationalism or Protestantism to the Catholic Faith, ask them why they rejected, and sometimes with supreme contempt, the teaching of the Church? Most of them will answer that they were ill-informed in regard to that teaching; many, that they were wholly ignorant of it.

If such was the religious ignorance of unbelievers as earnest as Maine de Biran, Augustin Thierry, and Droz, what must we think of the ordinary run of infidels? It is a fact, of which the infidel press alone gives mournful evidence, that the generality of them do not even suspect what the Catholic Religion may be. Ignorance in religious matters is truly a phenomenon.

Still a certain number of men are to be met with among infidels who are not ignorant of Catholic belief so far as this. They have some notion of the Christian Revelation and of the doctrines which it contains, they even find things in the life and teaching of the Church which command their admiration, but, seen under a false light, one point or other of the Catholic Creed or Catholic discipline stops them, and they remain in their unbelief. Some minds reject the Christian Faith because the mystery of the Trinity or of original sin shocks their reason. Ask them how they understand the doctrine of the Church on these two dogmas, which in our own opinion shed so valuable a light over history and philosophy, and you will at once perceive that they attach to these great mysteries a sense really repugnant to reason, and which has nothing in common with the Catholic sense; men create phantoms for themselves, and then shrink from them in horror. How many infidels impute to the Church on the subject of original sin not only what she does not teach, but what she has formally condemned! Then they draw consequences from this travesty of the Catholic dogma which are really monstrous, and which, if they were legitimately deduced from it, would, I admit, suffice to refute it in the eyes of all reasonable beings. What just and generous soul, they exclaim, would not shudder at that necessary consequence of the dogma of original sin—that infants who die unbaptized are punished eternally in hell like the greatest criminals? Were such a consequence well founded, I confess that I should be deeply disturbed by it. But in what General Council, in what Papal Bull, in what Scriptural or traditional source, in the writings of what authorized theologian, have they seen that such is the bearing of the Catholic dogma? We most emphatically deny that the Church anywhere teaches that children who die with the sole taint of original sin are punished in the same way as men who have been guilty of grave personal sin, and who quit this life in impenitence; the Church does not even teach that such children are positively unhappy.*

There is a simple and supremely reasonable Catholic maxim, which is a kind of bugbear to many minds which in other respects seem to be well enough disposed toward the Church; it is the maxim—No salvation out of the Church. But I repeat that this is but a necessary application of the most evident principles of reason, as soon as men admit that there is a religion revealed by God; nevertheless, we frequently see learned men who reject Catholicism, alleging this maxim as their excuse—they discover in it, what no Catholic theologian has ever seen, the wholesale and blind condemnation of all who do not belong to the external communion of the Church. Were such the meaning of this dogma, I do not hesitate to declare that it would be as absurd as it is odious; but thank God, it bears no such interpretation. Sometimes it is a simple point of Catholic discipline which disturbs and arrests certain minds. They only half understand it—they only know it according to the estimation of persons who are hostile, or at least strangers, to the Church; but there they stop and gravely declare that, although Catholicism may have good points, it cannot be accepted as a whole.

How terrible a thing is prejudice! We Catholics

---

* The reader may consult *Les Dogmes Catholiques*, on the nature and consequences of original sin in this world and the next, etc., tom. ii. liv. ix.

are often reproached with obeying prejudices. I
admit that in some respects we do obey prejudices,
but as a celebrated controversialist of the seventeenth century* has remarked, there are reasonable
prejudices and prejudices which are extremely unreasonable. Ask those who were formerly unbelievers—but whose firm and generous faith now rejoices the Church of God—whether they were not
slaves of most blind prejudice, when, like you, they
rejected the Catholic Faith? You will see what their
answer will be. Why, then, do not you, who love
truth and admire Christianity, if certain difficulties
present themselves, ask an explanation from the
teachers of that great religion which, for eighteen
hundred years, has been the consolation and glory
of the greatest geniuses of whom the world can
boast?

Why do you not imitate the noble and generous
mind of whom I spoke just now—why not go as he
did and confide your doubts, your hesitations, your
difficulties, to one of your brethren whose charge it
is to explain the teaching of this religion? What is
there opposed to your dignity in such a course?
Listen to the confessions of Droz, deploring the
fault he committed in seeking to escape from his
ignorance and his doubts without having consulted
any one: "When I wished to begin the examination of Christianity, I had been so much accustomed

---

* Pellisson.

to rely on my own light and guidance, that in my presumptuous ignorance I sought counsel of none to direct my researches. It is easy to see the utility of religion—its benefits are before our eyes; but instruction is necessary for the consideration of religion in itself, and to bring its truths home to ourselves. It was indispensable that a man who had been enlightened by its study should supply the light of which I was devoid. I knew a priest held in universal veneration; in my eagerness to escape from doubt I decided that I would see him the very next morning. . . . I opened my heart to him; I revealed to him my thoughts, my agitation, my desires, in all sincerity. I finished by saying to him: ' I owe to the proofs afforded by my feelings, the desire that religion should be true. Finish by conveying to my understanding the entire conviction which my heart craves. But if, instead of seeking to convince my reason, you command me to believe —if I must sacrifice the noblest gift I have received from Heaven—I have nothing more to ask you, we cannot understand one another.' "* Thanks to the instructions of the priest, this suspicious rationalist soon learnt that the Christian Faith does not sacrifice reason, but takes it for granted, purifies, strengthens, extends, and elevates it; he understood that Faith demands but one sacrifice, the sacrifice of pride, which he confounded with reason.

* *Aveux d'un Philosophe Chrétien*, pp. 65, 66.

CHAPTER V.

Causes of Religious Ignorance—It is often Voluntary, Culpable Ignorance—Levity and Moral Indifference of most Infidels.

IT is a wide-spread opinion in these days that error is not culpable, and that no one is responsible for the religious ignorance in which he lives. This opinion is supremely absurd, and shows too plainly the general decline of reason. Were it true, we should be obliged to declare that man is not a free agent, and that the truth has no claim upon his understanding. Our understanding, considered in itself, and apart from the will, is undoubtedly not free, but by its nature it is under the command of the will ; it is placed under the direction of the will and participates in its freedom. Let it never be forgotten that the will is the central power and ruler of the soul, that from the will the whole soul must receive its impulse and direction, that it is made to rule and direct the movements of the understanding as well as the movements of the feelings and affections—everything must depend upon the will, and the will is responsible for everything. Therefore, it cannot be too often repeated, it is the will that really makes the man. Let no one say that all conditions of the understanding, all ignorance in matters of religion, are things indifferent in themselves; our intellectual state depends in a very great measure upon our will, and the ignorance of which we are speaking may be voluntary, and consequently culpable. Man is bound to know the truth, to adhere to it, to submit to it; whoever wills not seriously and sincerely to make use of the means at his disposal to arrive at the truth, fails in his duty, and deserves punishment for his ignorance and his errors.

All ignorance of the religion revealed by God is assuredly not culpable. There are many souls to whom it is morally impossible to recognize the truth of the Church's teaching, either by reason of the condition in which they are living, or the atmosphere of prejudice which enveloped their early education, or of other circumstances absolutely independent of their will. God will not condemn these souls for that of which they are ignorant. Pius IX. recently wrote as follows to the Bishops of Italy: "We know and you know that they who are unavoidably ignorant of our most Holy Religion, and who, carefully observing the natural law and the precepts engraved by God in the hearts of all men, and willing to obey God, lead an honest, upright life, may, with the help of Divine light and grace, acquire eternal life; for God, who perfectly sees, searches, and knows the minds, souls, thoughts, and actions of all men, in his sovereign goodness and clemency, permits not that he who is not guilty of a voluntary fault should suffer eternal punishment."* It is a question of sincerity of which God is the judge.

But religious ignorance frequently depends on moral causes which must be studied, and this study will afford us occasion to penetrate more profoundly into the mystery of unbelief. Infidelity is a complex fact in which all the powers of the soul have a share. As we proceed, we shall be more and more convinced of this fundamental truth. We will begin by pointing out a general condition of the soul very common among unbelievers; next, we will show by what means many souls descend all the steps of unbelief till they lose themselves in Materialism, or perish in the helplessness of scepticism, or the aberrations of Pantheism. We will then return to the consideration of the moral obstacles which the Christian Faith meets with in the souls of the better class of infidels—of those who admit the fundamental dogmas of natural religion.

Levity of mind, moral dissipation, a culpable indifference to religion, is the ordinary source of religious ignorance and one of the most common causes of infidelity. What are the greater number of men who do not believe doing? What is the

---

* Encyclical Letter to the Cardinals, Archbishops, and Bishops of Italy. August 10, 1863.

usual condition of their souls? The Apostle St. John wrote to the first disciples of the Gospel: "Love not the world, nor the things that are in the world. . . . All that is in the world is the concupiscence of the flesh, and the concupiscence of the eyes, and the pride of life."* The world, in the language of Scripture, denotes men "who prefer visible and transitory things to those that are invisible and eternal."† This world ever exists, and although the triple concupiscence which the Apostle points out has in some respects diminished during the long reign of the Christian Faith, it still displays itself in the world, and still brings forth therein the fruit of death. Are not the pleasures of sense, riches, honors, the sole object of desire and pursuit to the ordinary run of unbelievers? Material interests, considered under their diverse forms, absorb them wholly. They occupy themselves only with perishable goods; this present life is everything to them. Probably they do not deny that there is a future life, but they think nothing about it; it is an item which does not enter into their calculations. To succeed in the world, to satiate themselves with riches, pleasure, and, if possible, with glory, or at any rate with honors, is their sole care. Some give themselves up with a kind of frenzy to sensual enjoyment, a great number exercise a kind of half restraint upon themselves,

---

* 1 John ii. 15, 16.
† Bossuet, *Traité de la Concupiscence*, chap. i.

and at least respect decency, though their view extends not beyond the narrow horizon of this earth. With such dispositions, men are capable of sinking to the lowest depths of degradation, but they will not raise themselves to the heights of the moral order to seek the light of truth. Such men as these do not even dream of studying religion.

Pascal said of the few infidels of his time: "We know well enough how men of this kind act. They think they have made great efforts at self-instruction if they have spent a few hours in reading the Scriptures, and have questioned some ecclesiastic on the truths of Faith. Afterward they boast of having made a fruitless search in books and among men. But, in truth, I cannot refrain from telling them, as I have often done, that such negligence is intolerable. The trifling interests of some stranger are not in question here; the stake is ourselves and our all."* "This negligence in a manner which concerns themselves, their eternity, their all, irritates more than it moves me; it astonishes me, it alarms me. To me it is monstrous."† What would the religious and austere solitary of Port Royal say if he lived in our days? It is no longer a question with the multitude of unbelievers of employing some hours in reading the Scriptures and questioning some ecclesiastic on the truths of Faith; they read nothing, they question no one,

---

* *Pensées*, part ii. art. 2: Necessité d'étudier la Religion.
† *Ibid.*

they take no thought of religion. There is a levity and indifference about them inexplicable in reasonable beings. "There must be strange disorder in a man's nature who can live in such a state, still more when he can pride himself on it."* And yet the greater number do really pride themselves on it. They despise us who believe; they denounce us as the enemies of reason, as men whose understandings are enslaved; whilst they look upon themselves as reason personified, claim for themselves alone liberty of thought, and proudly call themselves free-thinkers. From the time of La Bruyère infidels have called themselves *esprits forts;* this title called forth from the immortal author of *Les Caractères* the following reflection: " Do our *esprits forts* know that they are called thus in irony?† God forbid that I should wish to offend any one, but I cannot help seeing the most bitter irony in the name of free-thinkers as given to infidels. It is a fact that the generality of them think neither freely nor servilely; they do not think at all. Permit me to say frankly that there are infinitely more free-livers than free-thinkers among the enemies of the Christian Faith. If some few (and they are the exception) really think, I know of nothing less free than their thoughts; they are the slaves of the blindest and most absurd prejudices; they accept, with a truly blind faith, all the judgments which condemn Christianity. An infidel ex-

* Pascal. † *Les Caractères*, chap. xvi.

amining the bases of the Christian Religion, sincerely, without prepossession, with conscientious freedom, is the rarest thing in the world; when a man has done that, he is very near renouncing infidelity and embracing the Faith. But, I repeat, this multitude of worshippers of free examination, and these so-called free-thinkers examine nothing and never think for themselves. They repeat lofty maxims, write pompous formulæ, for the most part like parrots, and without attaching any meaning to them; this is the power and freedom of their thought in the domain of morals and religion. They affirm with imperturbable assurance that they are for the independence of reason, for the emancipation of the human mind, for progress, for the liberty of nations; according to them, the Catholic Faith is the antithesis of these beautiful and noble things. But do not ask them what they mean by the independence of reason, the emancipation of the human mind, and other articles of the rationalist programme; they are words which they repeat by heart and without having ever examined their true meaning. Above all, do not ask them in what the Catholic Faith, which is professed by the most independent, purest, and most eminent men of our days, as it was in the days of St. Augustine—do not ask them in what that Faith opposes the freedom of reason and shackles social progress. They have never thought of it; they will give you no other answer than the eternal sing-song of accusations a hundred times refuted, and formulæ as new as the formula which comprises all the religious science of the disciples of Mohammed : 'God is God, and Mohammed is his prophet.'"

We will close this chapter with one general observation. The meaning of words, must be restored. What man in his senses would say that moral freedom consists in exemption from the rule of virtue ? How, then, can men place intellectual liberty in exemption from the rule of truth ? For pity's sake, do not confound liberty with libertinism. There is a libertinism of thought as well as a libertinism of morals. To live regardless of the law of virtue is moral libertinism ; to think and speak without regard for the law of Truth is intellectual libertinism.

We will now see whither either one or the other may lead.

CHAPTER VI.

Materialism—On what it Rests—The Soul Materialized—How the Soul arrives at this State, and what Moral Treatment must be Followed to Raise it from this Degradation.

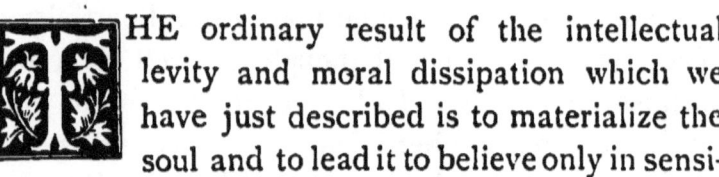HE ordinary result of the intellectual levity and moral dissipation which we have just described is to materialize the soul and to lead it to believe only in sensible realities. There is a twofold materialism—a dogmatic materialism which denies positively the existence of the soul and of God, and a practical materialism which denies neither the one nor the other expressly, but neglects and forgets them both. The moral condition, of which we have just spoken, cannot be distinguished from this practical materialism. We will now speak of dogmatic materialism, properly so called.

This materialism, which for a short time was ignominiously driven from the schools of infidel philosophy, has reappeared in the last few years, and has again acquired considerable influence. It is daily gaining ground in the domain of natural science, and many cultivated minds are ranging themselves under its banner. Now materialism is radical infidelity—it is the denial of the very foundation on which all religion rests, and on which the Christian Faith in particular must take its stand. How can a soul come to ignore and deny its own existence? How can it sink to this intellectual and moral degradation? The key to this mystery must be sought for in human liberty, which is the principle of all degradation and all elevation. We are free and imperfect beings; we may refuse our adhesion to truths of the moral order, and our soul may so far blind itself—not all at once, but by dint of a thousand weak and base acts—that at length it will come to ignore God, and no longer be able to discern itself. Men reach this point by two roads: by libertinism of life, and also, whilst preserving a comparatively virtuous exterior, by that religious indifference which enervates the best part of the soul and ends by extinguishing its life.

Our soul has a direct and immediate view of itself—it has a perception of itself, the manifestations of its life, its understanding, its sensibility, and its will; it perceives God and the moral order by evidence which seems irresistible. How then is materialism possible? It arises from the moral condition of the soul, it comes from this, that the state of our understanding depends in great measure on the state of our will and affections. All our faculties are mutually affected, and exercise an incessant action upon one another. Nothing is easier than to refute a materialist, but it is not so easy to cure him. This cure is only possible by means of a moral treatment which is occasionally very painful.

There are souls so buried in matter, so materialized, that the realities of the moral world have no longer any meaning to them, but appear to them the most inexplicable chimera. The most sublime religious symbols reveal absolutely nothing to them: in the most touching ceremonies of religion they behold merely external things, having no moral significance. A Russian of great distinction, who was converted a few years ago to the Catholic Faith, attests this of himself. M. Schouvaloff had in his youth lost all religious belief; not only did he no longer believe the Gospel, but he no longer recognized the existence either of God or of his own soul. Teachers of philosophy had confirmed him in his denial of the Truth. He passed several years in this state. In the history of his life, he says: "As I finish the account of this first part of my spiritual existence, I ask myself how it happened that neither my heart nor my mind was ever touched, when, during my sojourn in Italy, and particularly in Rome, I happened to be present at religious ceremonies. I cannot comprehend my indifference in this respect, nor how it happened that no serious idea ever came to me—to me who believed myself to be a thoughtful man—at the sight of things that had been objects of veneration for so many centuries, and that to men belonging to all classes of society, to every degree of intelligence. It is true that I never entered a church except out of curiosity or from some other frivolous motive, but still I went into the churches; I was present at glorious and beautiful ceremonies—my eyes were sometimes arrested by ancient sculptures or magnificent pictures, the figures of which, seen through clouds of incense, appeared animated with life; everywhere was to be seen the image of thy Holy Mother, surrounded with innumerable *ex voto*, tokens of hope, of sorrow, of gratitude, and of love; the most profound feelings of the heart had left their traces on her altars. Moreover, I heard words, sublime in their simplicity, mingling with the music of angels; the air of the Basilicas appeared to me to be impregnated with the sentiment of Faith; here, a whole people listened motionless to the voice of the preacher; there, the faithful were confessing their sins; others, with silent devout recollection, were receiving the Divine Body; prostrate priests adored the Sacred Host; an old man, the Father of Christians washed the feet of a few poor men, or gave his benediction to the city and to the world. . . . And in presence of these grand spectacles not a thought, not a question! I beheld them with the indifference of idiotcy. . . . One sense was wanting—the spiritual sense, the divine sense! My body was present, but my soul was elsewhere, . . . it slept."*

This is truly the condition of a materialized soul ; in it the moral sense is, as it were, extinct. Still, the root of this sense is alive, but is stifled by foreign elements. To restore its vigor, these elements must be removed, and the soul must be replaced in its true position. This is the object of the moral treatment of which I was speaking just now.

Plato was perfectly well acquainted with materialized minds; they abounded in pagan society. He has depicted them in several passages of his *Dialogues*, but particularly in the celebrated allegory of the cavern. The great moralist compares this visible world to a subterranean cave, in which men who have been in chains since infancy behold the shadows of objects through an opening and by the pale glimmer of a fire ; the captives imagine that these shadows are the only realities. "Now see," continues Plato, " what must naturally happen if they be delivered from their chains and cured of their error. Let one of these captives be unbound: let him be compelled to stand up at once, to turn his head, to walk, and to turn to the light. He will do all this with infinite trouble ; the light will hurt his eyes, and dazzle him so as to prevent his discerning the objects whose shadows he formerly beheld. What think you might he reply to him

* *Ma Conversion et ma Vocation*, by P. Schouvaloff, Barnabite, pp. 81-83. Paris, 1859.

who should tell him that up to this time he had seen only phantoms, but that now he has more real objects, objects more approaching to the truth, before his eyes? Suppose he were now pulled out of the cavern and dragged by a rude steep path to the light of the sun, what a punishment would it be to him! how great would be his fury! And when he should have reached the light of day, would not his eyes be dazzled by the brightness? Could he see anything of the crowd of objects which we call real beings? At first he would not be able to do so. Doubtless time would be necessary to accustom him to it." But when he had become accustomed to the sight of objects, and to the contemplation of the sun which gives them light, "if he happened to call to mind his first dwelling, the companions of his slavery, and the idea which they had there of wisdom, would he not rejoice in his own change? would he not compassionate their misfortune? Most assuredly he would. Do you think he would still be jealous of the honors, praise, and rewards given to him who was most prompt in seizing the shadows as they passed, or who called to mind most accurately which shadows went before, which followed, which went together, and thus was the most skilful in guessing the time of their appearance; or that he envied their condition who were most powerful and most honored in that prison? Would he not prefer passing his life, as is related of Achilles by Homer, in the service of a poor laborer, and suffer everything rather than resume his former condition, with its illusions? I doubt not that he would be ready to suffer everything rather than again live in that manner. . . . Well, my dear Glaucus, that is the precise image of our human state. The subterraneous cave is this visible world; the fire by which it is lighted is the light of the sun; the captive who soars to a higher region and who contemplates it is the soul raising itself to the sphere of intelligence."*

The materialized soul delights in this kingdom of shadows, which it takes for the only realities, and is irritated by any proposal to quit this world of phantoms. Only at the price of a generous effort can it be snatched from them. The fulfilment of a moral condition must be the first step; the soul must purify itself and disengage itself as much as possible from the mass of gross images which defile its sight and hinder it from contemplating the true light. In the *Phædo*, Socrates, discoursing on his approaching death, and seeking to console his friends, defines the purification of the soul to be a kind of anticipated death. " Does not the purification of the soul," he says, " consist in separating it as much as possible from the body; in accustoming it to be shut up in itself, to be recollected in itself, and to live as much as possible . . . alone and in itself, disengaged from the shackles of the body?

* *Republ.* lib. vii. 514-518.

... Without the least doubt this is so."* "Now what is death," adds Socrates, "if not the complete separation of the soul and body? The philosopher who seeks to purify his soul exercises himself in dying, and philosophy is an apprenticeship of death."† The illustrious sage of Athens had but a glimpse of this sublime thought, which was to be fully comprehended and realized — free from all admixture of error — by Christianity alone.

Plato recognizes three distinct principles in the soul of man: the superior or rational part of the soul is the seat of the understanding; the inferior part is the seat of sensation and material pleasures; the middle part is the seat of passions somewhat more elevated, such as anger, pride, and ambition.‡ For the man who seeks truth he teaches the necessity of subjecting the lower and middle parts of the soul to the superior, so that, free from all shackles, it may more easily turn to the contemplation of that which is. "Have you not yet remarked," says Socrates, "how far the sagacity of those men reaches to whom is given the name of clever rogues? With what penetration does their little soul (τὸ ψυχάριον) seize on the things to which it is turned. Its sight is by no means weak, but as they constrain it to serve their malice, the

---

* *Phædo*, 67.
† *Ibid.* Cicero and the Neoplatonicians reproduced this maxim.
‡ *Republ.* lib. ix. 580, 581.

more penetrating it is the more hurtful it is. This is most true. But take these same souls from childhood, cut and pare away all that the passions of lust have deposited therein, loosen them from the heavy masses attached to the pleasures of the table and similar luxuries, take away the weight which depresses the glance of the soul to inferior things — then if the same glance in the same souls, freed from these obstacles, is turned toward the things that are true, (εἰς τὰ ἀληθῆ,) it will behold them with the same penetration with which it now beholds these things to which it is turned."*

The faculty of knowing God and moral truths is implanted in man ; but it is weakened, paralyzed in its movements, turned away from its object, by the weight of sensual passions or by material prepossessions. To restore to this noble faculty its power of soaring on high, and to enable it to turn toward its true object, it is necessary to combat these passions and to triumph over these strange prepossessions. Man must be purified by mortification. Those who do not purify themselves spend their lives in miserably passing from the lower to the middle region of the soul, and in falling back again from the middle to the lower region, without ever raising themselves to that where God manifests himself. "Men who know neither wisdom nor virtue, who are always taken up with festivities

* *Republ.* lib. vii. 519.

and other sensual pleasures, necessarily sink to the lowest region, (κάτω;) thence they raise themselves to the middle region, (πρὸς τὸ μεταξὺ,) and pass their lives in wandering between the two. But to traverse these two regions in order to look upon that which is really on high, and to raise themselves to it, this is what they never do. Therefore they have never been filled with the possession of that which truly is, nor have they ever tasted a pure and solid joy. Bent down toward the earth, like animals whose eyes are ever fixed upon their food, they give themselves up brutally to good cheer and love; they dispute among themselves for the enjoyment of these pleasures, turn their arms against one another, and end in mutual slaughter. . . . You have just drawn to the life the condition of the greater number of men. Does not the same thing necessarily occur with regard to that part of the soul where courage resides —when ambition, seconded by jealousy, the spirit of strife by violence, and a savage disposition by anger, drive man — without reflection or discernment—to pursue a false plenitude of honor and victory, and afterward to the satisfying of his resentment? The same thing must necessarily happen."* How many men run after this false plenitude of honor and victory, and, willing captives, know not how to surmount the narrow frontiers of that cavern which can only offer them shadows!

* *Republ.* lib. ix. 586.

It is assuredly not absolutely necessary that the soul should be freed from the yoke of passions and interests before it can recognize God and the moral order, but it has need of a certain degree of purification to raise itself to that superior world and to attach itself thereto by a firm adhesion of the understanding. When a soul has attained this moral condition, it must, by an act of the will, unfold its divine faculty, and direct it on the object for which the soul is made. This is a movement which purification renders easy, and which completes the education of the soul. What is the use of the organ of sight if men do not make use of it, or if it is ill-directed? "In the evolution which is given to the soul," says Plato, once more, "the whole art consists in turning it in the easiest and most beneficial manner. The question is not to bestow on it the faculty of sight, it has that already; but its organ is in a bad direction, it does not look in the right direction. . . . The faculty of knowledge . . . never loses its power, only it becomes useful and advantageous, or useless and hurtful according to the direction which is given to it, (ὑπὸ τῆς περιαγωγῆς.)"* This is the real supreme importance of the part which the will bears in knowledge. Would that those poor souls who deny God and ignore themselves would seriously reflect upon it!

* *Republ.* lib. vii. 518.

CHAPTER VII.

Scepticism—In what it consists—Different Causes of Scepticism.

HOW few souls are there, in these days, who preserve their equilibrium and their uprightness, affirming what ought to be affirmed, denying what ought to be denied, abstaining from judging where it is right so to abstain! Aristotle has defined virtue to be the middle between two vices, the too much and the too little.* I do not accept this definition in its full extent, but it is frequently no less applicable in the intellectual than in the moral life. Sometimes men foolishly seek to raise themselves, alone and without support, above human nature; sometimes they sink below that same nature by falling miserably into materialism or scepticism. How many minds are in perpetual oscillation between these two extremes, slipping now on one side, now on the other, without power to fix themselves in the just medium which reason prescribes!

Scepticism often depends on a moral condition similar to that which engenders and nourishes materialism; occasionally, however, it arises from

* Ethic. Nicom. ii. 6.

other causes. I am now speaking of moral universal scepticism, of that state of mind which denies nothing positively, but at the same time does not affirm any truth of the moral order, whether natural or supernatural; in which a man doubts the existence of God, of his own soul, of all religious principles. With some men, universal doubt is the result of a false system of philosophy carried out to its extreme point, but this is an exception which we need not specially notice. Even in minds that give themselves up to philosophical studies and are sincerely prepossessed in favor of the truth, scepticism is rarely the logical product of a false method; it almost always depends on other causes; it springs for the most part from a monstrous and bitter deception. It is this deception which directly engenders intellectual despair; but in this it is assisted by moral dispositions which indicate an unhealthy condition of the soul. Scepticism is a weakness of the will and of the understanding. It is the younger son of pride, if I may so speak. Pride begins with a ridiculous self-sufficiency and ends in despair. This is, in one word, the history of many sceptics of lofty and earnest intelligence. In this way, as we have already seen, St. Augustine fell into scepticism. Disdaining the Christian Faith, he at first imagined that he should be able to discover everything by reason alone; when deceived in this presumptuous confidence, that noble genius recoiled upon itself, and took up the belief that the human understanding is powerless to attain a certain knowledge of truth. How many infidels, in our own days and under our own eyes, have gone through this same experience! Their reason, jealous of a false independence, sought to walk alone to the conquest of all truths, and rejected with disdain the support of Divine Authority. And in what did this course generally end? For the most part in miserable discouragement and bitter despair. I will content myself with recalling the example of Theodore Jouffroy, one of the most eminent philosophers of the school of French rationalists. Jouffroy had received a Catholic education, but his belief was weak and unenlightened, and vanished at the first breath of rationalistic teaching. His young and ardent mind, seduced by the false promises of infidel philosophy, was persuaded that it was about to find, in that philosophy, the clear and definitive solution of all problems. "My mind," wrote the disappointed philosopher at a later period, "was persuaded that on entering upon the study of philosophy it was about to encounter a regular science, which, after having pointed out its end and the process by which to attain it, would conduct me by a sure and well-defined road to the certain knowledge of those things which are of surpassing interest to man. In one word, my understanding, excited by its necessities and enlarged by the teaching of Christianity, had ascribed to philosophy the grand object, the vast frame-work, the sublime bearing of a religion. . . . Such had been my hope ; and what did I find? The struggle which had awakened the slumbering echoes of the faculty, and which had turned the heads of all my fellow-students, had for its object—its sole object—the question of the origin of ideas. I could not recover from my astonishment that men should occupy themselves with the origin of ideas with as much ardor as if the whole of philosophy was contained in it,* *and yet leave on one side man, God, the world, and the relations which unite them to the enigma of the past and the mysteries of the future, and to many other gigantic problems on which they did not conceal their scepticism.* All philosophy seemed to be buried in a hole where there was no air, and in which my soul, recently exiled from Christianity, was stifled ; yet the authority of the teachers and the fervor of their disciples impressed me, and I dared not show either my surprise or my disappointment."†

Jouffroy soon became one of the most distinguished masters of that philosophy which assumed to be the supreme personification of reason. His

---

* It must not be forgotten that in Rationalism, philosophy takes the place of religion, and ought consequently to fulfil the task of religion.

† *Noveaux Mélanges Philosophiques*, by Theodore Jouffroy, published by H. Damiron, pp. 118-121. Paris, 1842. The words *printed in italics* have disappeared from the published copies, but they are to be found in the rare copies which have escaped the mutilation which the tardy and useless prudence of alarmed Rationalism has made this work undergo.

personal researches could not fill up the void which the loss of faith had produced in his soul. All religious certainty had disappeared from his mind. He became a sceptic. God, man, the world, their mutual relations, all those grand problems which every intelligent soul necessarily proposes to itself, remained obscure enigmas to him. Listen to the philosopher telling, with the accent of despair, the impression which the sight of the places where he had once had the happiness to live as a Christian made upon his afflicted soul. He says: " I found myself once more under the roof where I had passed my childhood, in the midst of those who had brought me up so tenderly, in the presence of objects which had struck my eyes, touched my heart, affected my understanding, in the happy days of my early life. . . . All was unchanged except myself. The Church, where the holy mysteries were celebrated with the same devotion; the fields, the woods, the fountains which were still blessed in the spring-time; the house where, on the appointed day, an altar of flowers and foliage was still erected; the Curé, who had instructed me in the Faith and who had grown old, was still there—still firm in his belief; all who surrounded me had the same heart, the same soul, the same hope in faith. I alone had lost it. *I alone lived without knowing how or why. I alone, so learned, knew nothing. I alone was empty, agitated, deprived of* *light, blind, and restless."** This is what Rationalism had effected in an understanding naturally so powerful and enlightened.

These last words of Jouffroy, so profoundly mournful, remind me of the observation of another philosopher who was also for some time an infidel, but who returned at last to the Faith of his childhood. M. Droz says : "I was often astonished to see illustrious philosophers less enlightened on the most important subjects than humble Christians. Is it not shameful that sages should consume long watches in seeking what has been long ago found? Philosophers discuss the question as to what is man's destination upon earth; they plunge into subtleties, they exhaust themselves in declamations more or less eloquent, and in the meanwhile, a good Christian woman would say to them: 'God has created us to love him and to worship him, and to make us one day participate in his felicity. Here we are in a place of probation where duties are imposed upon us; we may fulfil them or we may transgress them. After this short life, according as we shall have obeyed or resisted the will of our Father, he will reward us because he is good, or he will punish us because he is just.' If philosophers do not confine themselves to the develop-

---

* Work quoted by M. Guizot in his *Méditations et Etudes Morales*, Préface. Paris, 1852.

ment of these words in treating the same subject, they *unteach* us the truth."*

Jouffroy was unable to recover from his fall into scepticism. This proud philosopher concludes his works by charging philosophy with absolute impotence; he ends by declaring with bitter sadness that philosophy, which in his idea is the same thing as Rationalism, raises and brings to light a multitude of questions, none of which it is able to resolve. What a lesson is this! "Men begin," as I have said elsewhere, "by proclaiming the omnipotence of human reason, and end by accusing it of utter weakness. This is surely the well-deserved chastisement of pride, which in its delirium refuses to accept the conditions which God has imposed upon our nature, and disdainfully rejects the hand which alone can save us. Neither so high nor so low is the teaching of good sense, and the teaching of Catholic philosophy. Rationalism is neither reason nor philosophy; it is the mortal enemy of both; it compromises them and destroys them by its exaggerations and its foibles."†

The causes of scepticism are complex; it is not produced in the same way in all minds that are attacked by this terrible malady. In the case of most infidels, it is not the result of a serious search after truth, but of an ill-directed search; it is the fruit of levity, of dissipation, of indolence of the

* *Aveux d'un Philosophe Chrétien*, pp. 32, 33.
† *Les Dogmes Catholiques*, tom. iii. p. 199. Paris, 1861.

will, or of a false direction of the understanding. Many Christians who are not familiar with psychological studies ask themselves if scepticism is really possible, and are astonished that earnest men can fall into such error. I can understand this blessed ignorance of evil. The faculties in a Christian soul are in equilibrium; they are maintained in their vigor and in their normal state; scepticism, which is the overthrow and ruin of our moral and intellectual nature, is an impossibility in such a condition. But let a man enter into himself and scrutinize his own thoughts, let him study attentively the history of those souls who are not settled in the truth by Faith, and he will soon be convinced that scepticism is unfortunately but too possible, and that it is easier to become the prey of this monster than people usually imagine. Let it never be forgotten that man is as free in his adhesion to truth as he is in his adhesion to virtue; in both orders it is possible to fall away; men may reject what is true as they may reject what is good; they may hesitate and vacillate in affirming what is true, as well as in practising what is good.

All truths, even those which we call evident and which in reality are so, present a dark side to human reason; man, according to the saying of Montaigne, sees the whole of nothing. Even in the purely natural order, every object of human thought presents two faces—two sides; one, clear, luminous, evident; the other, dark and cloudy. I see a man; I affirm his existence; I affirm that he is a being composed of two distinct substances, body and soul. This affirmation rests on evidence. But when I affirm the existence of the body, when I affirm the existence of the soul, do I know which is the precise object of this twofold affirmation? I know it in a certain degree. I know which are the proper characteristics of the body; I know which are the essential properties of the soul; I see clearly that they are two distinct substances. But if I am asked to state in clear and forcible terms in what the essence of the human body consists, what constitutes its life, what the action of the organs of the body is, and how it is produced; if I am asked to define with the utmost precision the essence of my own soul, and to explain the play of all its faculties, I confess that I have no answer to give. I could certainly give a few explanations and elucidations, but I should soon come to a point before which I should be obliged to pause, and a grain of sand stops me as much as man. What philosopher durst flatter himself that he knows thoroughly, and in all their parts, those things the reality of which he affirms? A mysterious obscurity hangs over all our knowledge. One of the leaders of French Rationalism has said with great truth, "In science, as often as we make any advance, we find an abyss; only weak minds believe that they can explain all and understand all."*

* Jules Simon, *La Religion Naturelle*, p. 45. Paris, 1856.

If nature herself, bounded, limited, finite as she is, conceals depths which our minds cannot fathom, must not God, the Infinite Being, be full of obscurity to us? No truth can be more easily demonstrated than the existence of God. But what incomprehensible things are there in the nature of that God whose existence reason demonstrates! Jules Simon, judging in this respect of the pretensions to omniscience which many of his companions in Rationalism set up, says: "More humiliated by what is wanting to us than intoxicated by that which we are permitted to discover, the first word we shall pronounce when we speak of God is *incomprehensibility*. Human pride, and we must also say philosophical pride, revolts at this word. We are willing enough to admit that religion speaks of the incomprehensibility of God, and every one knows that the Catholic Religion proclaims a hidden God—an incomprehensible God; but it would seem that the very end of philosophy is to explain all mysteries, to render all ideas precise, to carry everywhere the light of reason, and to accustom the human mind to believe only what it can prove and understand. We might say that Bayle's proverb, 'Understanding is the measure of belief,' is the very motto of philosophy. To believe without proof or to believe without understanding appears to human reason to be at most only two different modes of abdicating its claims. . . . . These commonplaces cannot stand examination. In science, the question is not to attain what we wish, but to attain what we can. No doubt the essence of philosophy consists in believing nothing without proof; but when the existence of a being is once proved, are we to renounce our belief in that existence on the pretext that the nature of that being is incomprehensible to us? . . . These data are so simple and natural, that when we reflect on them we know not how to explain the pretensions to omniscience which certain schools have set up."* "If in nature herself," adds the philosopher, "that is to say, in what is necessarily limited and imperfect, we admit the existence of real mysteries unfathomable to human reason, by what mental aberration would we have the only perfect Being to be without abysses which our thoughts cannot penetrate?"† "My life is passed at the bottom of an abyss, in the midst of mysteries. I am surrounded by the unknown; I am myself ever unknown to my own mind, (in the sense in which we spoke just now.) In spite of all this I live in peace. I speak of science in pompous terms, and when I come to demonstrate the existence of God and am told that he is incomprehensible, I cry out and declare myself offended in my dignity as a human being and as a philosopher." ‡

No one could express this better. In these passages the author of *La Religion Naturelle* does but

* Ouv. cit. pp. 35, 36.   † *Ibid.* p. 38.   ‡ *Ibid.* p. 43.

declare a well-known truth—one which has been recalled and explained a hundred times by Christian philosophers, but it is a truth big with consequences and which has always more or less affrighted Rationalism.

This, then, is the condition of human reason. We meet with mystery even in the dogmas of natural religion—in things which seem the most familiar to us. What must we do in presence of that obscurity which in all our knowledge mingles constantly with the light? Must I deny, or abstain from affirming the existence of God because I can only comprehend his nature in part? It is undeniable that I can do so. The obscurity which accompanies light, and to which our intelligence is averse, makes this denial possible, and leaves me at liberty to give or refuse my consent to the known truth. All depends on the disposition of my will. We know what scepticism is. It will not accept a light mingled with shadows—it rejects the light out of fear and hatred of darkness. A reasonable man will not act thus. He admits the obscurity, which is inseparable from all knowledge; he admits it, not for itself, but on the authority of the light. He knows that he is not intended to understand everything. We are intelligent beings, no doubt, but we are also finite beings, and consequently the comprehension with which we are endowed is finite. Also, further, we are beings subject to trial; and this state of probation excludes the full light of day. We mistake the laws of our nature and of our actual condition if we deny the existence of God because his nature is incomprehensible to us. Such pride would be ridiculous were it not profoundly criminal.

Occasionally scepticism springs less from pride than from a false direction of the understanding. Some minds prefer to direct and arrest their attention to what is obscure, not only with regard to moral and religious truths, but to historical facts and questions of natural science; they will not look at the light, or scarcely glance at it, they fix their eyes only on the shadows. Is it astonishing if they do not see, or if they hesitate and grope their way along like the blind? We know many such minds. Things which are the most evident, the most solidly demonstrated, appear doubtful to them, because they do not see arguments, but pay attention to a thousand little difficulties in which their darkened reason perplexes itself, and ends by losing its way completely. Why not look on the side where light is?

We have said already that levity, indifference, apathy, generally helped and fed by the passions. is the most frequent cause of religious scepticism. Men do not love the truth; they do not desire it— they fear it and turn away from it as from an enemy. With such dispositions, without the special aid of God, how can they avoid becoming sceptics?

But let them not deceive themselves; such a scepticism is highly criminal, and the truth, from which they now fly, will one day find them out to their cost.

One, who had traversed all the phases of infidelity, has said: "The greatest benefit of religion is to save us from doubt and uncertainty. . . . All is uncertain, fugitive, and changeable, in a mind destitute of religious belief."* Change, instability, fluctuation, is a malady of the understanding as well as of the heart of man; faith cures us of this malady by fixing our mind upon truth and prohibiting doubt: those who do not believe are but too frequently its victims. "Therefore," says an Italian philosopher, "the Catholic precept is most wise which forbids us to admit a doubt of the known truth even for a single instant. The weakness and instability of the human mind are such, and so great, that however strong and solid our persuasion of the truth of any article of faith may be, there is not one with regard to which difficulties may not sometimes arise, capable of making a momentary impression on the mind; if men entertain this impression, doubting of the truth which they possess, they will by degrees acquire a habit of scepticism which will soon leave no belief intact. But if, on the contrary, they courageously resist these assaults—if they despise these involuntary clouds of the mind—by degrees the darkness will

* Maine de Biran, *Journal Intime*, p. 333.

disperse, calm will return, they will be able to smile at their doubts instead of thinking them formidable, and will wonder that they ever looked on them in a serious light. Sophistry sometimes assumes a specious and seductive aspect in the eyes of the understanding, as the passions do in the eyes of the heart; but if men are strong and do not yield to appearances, it will soon vanish away."*

* Gioberti, *Introduzione allo Studio della Filosofia*. From the French translation, t. iii. p. 182.

CHAPTER VIII.

Corruption of the Understanding—Sophistry and its Victims.

HE understanding may become corrupted as well as the heart, but this is a case of less frequent occurrence ; we have, however, signal examples of this corruption of the understanding in our day. This corruption is at once the root and the fruit of sophistry. I have no desire to go over the subject of modern sophistry, which my friend, Father Gratry, has treated in so masterly a manner ; but after having, in the words of this uncompromising religious writer, pointed out the evil, I will seek to indicate the remedy.

" The sophists of the eighteenth century attacked the Faith in the name of reason ; those of the nineteenth now attack reason itself. The sophists follow in the intellectual order the course which, according to Tacitus, they follow in the political order—they attack reasonable life in the same manner as they attack social life. ' They first attack power,' says Tacitus, 'in the name of liberty, and when power has been overcome they attack liberty itself.'* We see the same thing before our eyes in the intellectual order. At first they attacked the power and authority of Faith in the name of reason; now they attack the free and manifest light of reason. At first they rejected the Eternal Word illuminating the assembly of Christians with his revelations; now they attack the Word, who, as the eternal light of reason, enlightens every man coming into this world. . . . Such is the progress of intellectual decay.

"It is certain that *the absurd*, set forth daringly, openly, and without evasion, has sometimes a strange power. It has the fascination of a precipice. I know many instances of it. When a mind has once had the weakness to hesitate for an instant in presence of the visibly absurd, that mind is lost. As there is nothing more to expect, in the order of thought, from a mind which demands the demonstration of evidence, so there is nothing more to hope for from a mind which demands the refutation of the absurd, which is itself the evidence of error. Beyond evidence there is nothing to demonstrate; beyond the absurd there is nothing to refute.

"There philosophy stops. Then the mind, deprived of the support of evidence, and of the beacon-light of the absurd, quits the limits of reason, and abandons philosophy for sophistry. . . . And what

---

* "Ut imperium evertant libertatem præferunt; si perverterint, libertatem ipsam aggredientur."—*Annal* xvi. 22.

is sophistry? It is the process of a reason overthrown, which asks the demonstration of evidence, and which in the meanwhile denies evidence; which demands the refutation of the absurd, and which in the meanwhile affirms the absurd."*

It is not that, as in materialism and scepticism, the soul is simply hebetated or enfeebled; sophistry is the perversion and utter overthrow of the mind. All is reversed; the fundamental principles of reason are overthrown, and the understanding, as it were, uprooted, floats in darkness and feeds upon contradictions. Hegel is the great master of sophistry, as we stated before, on the subject of Pantheism. Hegel has founded in the midst of our Christian Europe a sophistry infinitely more dangerous than that of Gorgias and the other Greek sophists whom Socrates and Plato opposed. He has ruined innumerable minds. Father Gratry says once more: "When a mind under the influence of Hegelism, which is the most daring and at the same time the most radical form of sophistry, has once given way, and destroyed the two extreme limits of reason, which are evidence and the absurd, that mind—whatever may be its riches, its distinction, its natural qualities—that mind is lost. You can no longer reckon upon its judgment. To it assertion and contradiction are alike. It seeks contradiction methodically. Philosophy is now

* *Une Etude sur la Sophistique contemporaine*, by Père Gratry, pp. 114-126 Paris, 1851.

out of the question: the mind is occupied only with that sterile movement of thought of, for, or against, which Plato in the *Sophist* calls in derision 'enantiopoiology.'"*

This sophistry, the effects of which are before our eyes, springs directly from Pantheism; it is the necessary application of the only logic which that cloudy system has to show; which lays down as a thesis the identity of God and the world, of the necessary and the contingent, of the absolute and the relative, and thus terminates fatally in the confusion of truth and falsehood, good and evil, being and non-existence. Pantheism is the doctrine of universal identity or general confusion. In this pretended philosophy, light and darkness, day and night, are but one and the same thing. Hegel affirms this in express terms in his logic. It is the direct negation of reason, of what humanity in all times has always called reason.

For some years past Pantheism has in a remarkable degree lost its prestige in the philosophical schools; but it has poisoned the reason of Europe, and even in these days intelligent men, otherwise richly endowed, are attacked by its venom. Many minds are wholly corrupted; they have no principles left in virtue of what they call progress; that which is true to-day may be false to-morrow; they have no longer a single fixed point, and their reason, being truly uprooted, vacillates between an as-

* Ouv. cit. pp. 126, 127.

sertion and its contrary, and incessantly contradicts itself, whilst firmly believing in its own fidelity. Intellectual corruption is not the same in all sophists; but we are acquainted with several, regarded as oracles by a considerable portion of the unbelieving world, in whom reason appears to be totally overthrown.

How are such minds to be cured? I know of but two remedies—humility and the sincere love of truth. Contempt of truth is the characteristic of the sophist, and it is usually the fruit of moral and intellectual egotism—that is, of pride in its highest degree. The leader of contemporary sophistry himself warns us that the soul must strip itself of all love for being, truth, justice, God, in order to arrive at confounding being and non-being. Listen to the profound teaching of these words: "The formula, 'Being and non-being are identical,' appears so great a paradox that reason can scarcely regard it in a serious light. Doubtless no great effort of the mind is necessary to render the assertion, that being and non-being are the same thing, ridiculous, nor to deduce absurdities in its application. For instance, it may be maintained as a consequence of this principle, that it is the same thing whether my house, my goods, the air I breathe, this city, the sun, justice, the soul, God, are or are not. . . . In fact, philosophy is precisely that doctrine which teaches man to free himself from a multitude of special ends and points of view, and renders him independent of everything, so that it is absolutely indifferent to him whether things are or are not."*

Hegel agrees then with us ; the absolute indifference of the soul with respect to all things is, in his eyes as it is in ours, the source or nourishment of sophistry. Let this detestable source, then, be dried up and sophistry will disappear. Let this deadly indifference be replaced by the vivifying love of truth, justice, and goodness ; reason will then recover its uprightness, and the soul, quitting the cloudy abyss where it is struggling, will soar once again to the pure, serene regions of light.

* " In der That ist die Philosophie eben diese Lehre, den Menschen von einer unendlichen Menge endlicher Zwecke und Absichten zu befreien, und ihn dagegen gleichgültig zu machen, so dass ihm allerdings dasselbe sei, ob solche Sachen sind oder nicht."—Hegel, *Œuvres*, 2 edit. tom. vi. pp. 171, 172.

CHAPTER IX.

Unbelievers who admit the Fundamental Principles of Natural Religion—Causes of their Unbelief.

SOPHISTRY, scepticism, materialism, are all radical forms of infidelity, which attack reason as directly as Faith; that is to say, they aim at the total ruin of the moral man. We will again quote Father Gratry, who says: "We have frequently repeated, after Plato, Leibnitz, and others, that the mind of man may follow two contrary tendencies, by the one raising itself toward being, toward God, by the other, sinking toward nothingness; one is followed by philosophers, the other by sophists. Traces of these two tendencies are to be found in all ages; it is an intellectual imitation of the life or death of souls according as they ascend toward God, or depart from him of their own free will."* The infidelity which has been described in the three preceding chapters is the act of minds which, by a free and secret choice, descend toward nothingness and plunge themselves into darkness. No Christian age has ever witnessed so many souls given over to this spirit of darkness as the present.

* *Logique*, tom. i. pp. 124, 125.

Let not earnest men, who have retained some vigor, some moral uprightness, whether they are believers or unbelievers, deceive themselves; reason is in peril; in the midst of the astonishing material progress which this century realizes every day, and to which we give our willing admiration, reason, good sense, that something which is the support and necessary safeguard of society, is visibly lowered; the moral standard of men's minds has sunk in a manner which would alarm us, did we not hope in the invincible power of the Christian Faith.

How is it that the best among rationalists, those who join us in our struggles against sophists, obstinately reject this Faith, without which our civilization would soon sink into the abject grossness of materialism? How is it that learned men, who recognize a personal God infinitely good and infinitely wise, all-powerful and free, Creator of the world—how is it that they reject all positive intervention of this God in the government of the human race, that they deny the miraculous and supernatural order, understand not that marvellous, and, if I may be permitted to call it so, that *natural* effusion of infinite goodness in the Incarnation of Jesus Christ? We must endeavor to clear up this moral mystery.

From the moment men admit miracles they are no longer infidels, and in our European society they are very near being Christians. Now, is it conceivable that a learned man, whose mind is not corrupted, should recognize a personal and free God, the Master of the universe, and yet deny him the power of acting in the world as he pleases, according to the dictates of his wisdom and the inspirations of his love? Droz, who had been an infidel for a great part of his life, passes the following judgment on this incomprehensible prejudice: " Infidels have one fixed idea. They will have it that miracles are impossible. When I was but a Deist, I recognized the absurdity of those who pretended to impose limits on Divine Power. I will add that this age is too enlightened for the prejudice which refuses to admit miracles to subsist. The day will come when it will be a consequence of this simple evident truth: God is an Infinite Being."* Nevertheless, this prejudice, so manifestly contrary to reason, still maintains its ground.

We remarked, when relating the conversion of the philosopher Justin, that in the early ages of Christianity, pagans who were learned, and anxious to discover truth, generally admitted the Christian Faith from the moment that the idea of the true God, the Creator of the world, had fully taken possession of their understanding; the religion of Jesus Christ, with its mysteries, its institutions, its practices, appeared to the generous and grateful souls of these men a consequence and in some sort a natural application of the idea of a God in-

*Aveux d'un Philosophe Chrétien, p. 79.

finitely perfect, who is rather the Father than the Master of the human race. The knowledge of God and of his relations with the world led straight to the belief in the Incarnation of the Word and in all the ineffable inventions of the love of the Saviour of men.* There is not a single pagan philosopher mentioned in the early ages of the Church who rejected the Christian Faith after having accepted the true notion of God. Why is it otherwise in our days? How is it that we see earnest minds admit the natural, whilst they reject the supernatural part of the Christian Creed? This depends on certain moral dispositions.

After St. Augustine had studied in the school of Plato, he recovered himself nobly; he rose to things appertaining to the intelligible world, and found once more the spiritual and perfect God, who is the light of the world. But the Platonists had not instructed him in the true relations between God and the created universe; they did not know them. Still, in their school he had formed a sufficiently pure idea of God, though it was incom-

---

* "The Sacrament of the Eucharist," says Madame Swetchine, "is the noblest expression of a love which can brook no limit, no separation, no obstacle. By this adorable Sacrament we feel the presence of God in ourselves, his intimate union, not only with the spirit, but also with the flesh and blood. The love of God, Almighty as himself, could go no farther, but thus far it could go, and in mercy God has stopped only at its extreme limits. . . . The reality of our Lord's presence in the Holy Eucharist emanates almost necessarily from redemption, as the supreme consequence and highest development of infinite love. The Eucharist is the natural effect of a supernatural charity."—*Méditations et Prières*, pp. 212, 213 Paris, 1863.

plete and undefined. In this state he saw no difficulty in believing in the Word of whom Christianity speaks, but he could not understand the mystery of the Incarnation of the Word. And why did his mind recoil before this mystery? He tells us himself it was because he was governed by a pride which hindered him from recognizing and confessing the weakness, the failings, the moral miseries from which his soul was suffering.* When St. Augustine saw himself as he really was, with all the humiliations and all the necessities of his nature, then he understood the benefit of the Incarnation of the Word, and Jesus Christ appeared to him as the necessary Restorer of our fallen nature. Is it not possible that many rationalists are retained in unbelief by the same causes which retained St. Augustine? "You *will not* come to me," said the Word Incarnate himself to the Jews who rejected him.† The true root of unbelief is the will. It is pride, it is sensuality, it is egotism in some shape or other which hinders the will from turning toward Jesus Christ and fixing in sincerity the eye of the understanding on this adorable form. "How can you believe," said the Saviour to the Pharisees, who were proud of their vain wisdom—"How can you believe, who receive glory from one another, and the glory which is from God alone you do not seek?"‡ And once more: "Men loved darkness rather than the light, for their works were evil."§

* Conf. lib. vii. c. 20.   † John v. 40.   ‡ John v. 44.   § John iii. 19.

Human nature is still the same. St. Paul said that the Cross was a stumbling-block to the Jews and foolishness to the Gentiles. For God, the Master of the world, to lower himself, for the love of men, even to die upon a cross, was, in the eyes of egotism, an unspeakable absurdity. When men do not love, how can they understand what love is? When men refer everything to themselves, how can they comprehend the generous and admirable folly of devotion and sacrifice? The Cross of Jesus Christ has exalted human nature. It has become to all civilized nations the symbol of honor and of glory; and nevertheless it remains a stumbling-block and foolishness to infidels. When will they surmount the narrow boundaries of that egotism in which they waste away in sterile and delusive self-enjoyment? When will they comprehend that if we, who are evil, can give our life to save one of our brethren, God, who is Infinite Goodness, can empty himself, according to the expression of St. Paul, take the form of a servant, and die upon a cross, out of love for his children and to save them? A pure, devoted, humble soul has nothing to oppose to the Christian Faith, but beholds in it the most touching, and at the same time the most magnificent effusion of the love of God.

Rationalists, I well know, hide their unbelief under fair pretexts. Reason, they say, must not abdicate its sway; reason has prerogatives which it may not renounce. In Christians, they say, reason abdicates by submitting to a power foreign to itself and by accepting mysteries which it cannot understand on the authority of that power. I wish to believe that men are sincere when they speak thus, but we are so ingenious in deceiving ourselves when the sacrifice of some passion is in question. Ask Droz, Augustine Thierry, Maine de Biran, or any other of the numerous infidels who have recently returned to the Faith, whether they sacrificed one single prerogative of reason in submitting to the authority of the Church; they will answer, that they had certainly to sacrifice prejudices and passions, but that on becoming Christians they did but yield full obedience to reason. Why, then, speak of the abdication of reason, and of a power foreign to reason? Is God a stranger to reason? We Catholics bow before the authority of the Church, because we regard her as the representative and permanent organ of Jesus Christ, the Word made flesh; we believe this not blindly, not lightly, but because the proofs which establish it are evident to the eyes of reason. Faith is finite reason, obeying infinite reason, or the Word of God, in all things; what can be more just? what more worthy of us? We admit doctrines, it is true, which transcend reason and which reason can only half understand, but we accept them on the testimony of an authority whose title cannot be disputed. Besides, in things of the purely natural order, the human mind meets with obscurities, with unfathomable mysteries; why, then, should it take offence at mysteries of the supernatural order?

Jules Simon, one of the leaders of spiritualistic rationalism, speaks eloquently of the mysteries of the natural order, but condemns absolutely, in the name of reason, the mysteries of Christianity. This philosopher sees an essential difference between the incomprehensible and mystery in the Christian sense of the word. These are the incredible words which he has written on the subject in the first edition of his book, *La Religion Naturelle*: "If, in this explanation of the incomprehensible, propositions are enunciated which are not proved, which do not convey a precise meaning to the mind, and *which imply contradiction in terms, this new doctrine is that which properly constitutes mystery*. This doctrine is not only incomprehensible; besides this characteristic it has three others: it is affirmed without being demonstrated; it is not intelligible in its enunciation; it contains a formal contradiction."* All this is false, absolutely false, and in direct opposition to all the teaching of Catholic theology. Christian mysteries are all demonstrated; not in themselves, doubtless, but in revelation, the existence of which is verified by reason with an evidence which defies objection; all are intelligible in their enunciation, and no one has

---

* *La Religion Naturelle*, pp. 233, 234. The author has modified this language in the third edition of his work, but he has not corrected the idea which it expresses.

ever been able to discover the slightest contradiction in a single dogma of Christianity. Jules Simon knows nothing of our great theologians, who, nevertheless, deserve to be consulted by every earnest philosopher. He knows not that a science exists infinitely higher than the petty philosophy with which rationalism seeks to nourish superior minds, and that this science, which is called theology, consists precisely in the explanation of all those mysteries of which he speaks so lightly.* But at least he knows Leibnitz, for he has borrowed largely from him. Now Leibnitz establishes clearly that the Christian mysteries are not contradictory, that they do not contradict reason, that they are not contrary to any truth evidently recognized by reason ; that their enunciation presents a sufficiently intelligible meaning to the mind, and that, in short, all objections opposed to them may be solved. " That which is contrary to mysteries in us," says Leibnitz, " is not reason, or the natural light, or the natural sequence of truths ; it is corruption, it is error or prejudice, it is darkness."† This is what that great man thought of the contra-

---

* Relying on the works of the authorized interpreters of theology, we have ourselves attempted a thorough explanation of all the mysteries of the Catholic Creed. We do not pretend to have demonstrated those mysteries, but we think we have placed them in such a light, that, according to the expression of F. Lacordaire, " pride can only insult itself in despising them."
—See *Les Dogmes Catholiques*.

† *Essais de Théodicée. Discours de la Conformité de la Foi et de la Raison*, n. 61.

dictions which erring minds imagine they have discovered in the mysteries of Christianity.

Let people cease to set the prerogatives and dignity of human reason against the Christian Faith. We believe on good evidence; our faith has nothing in common with credulity. "There is a great difference," as Joubert well observes, "between credulity and faith; one is a natural defect of the mind, the other is a virtue; the first comes from our extreme weakness, the second has a mild and praiseworthy docility for its principle, quite compatible with strength, and which is even highly favorable to strength."* This docility, whence faith springs, is not contrary to our dignity; it is only contrary to our pride. "Let us be men with men," says Joubert once more, "but before God let us be always children; for in fact, we are but children in his eyes."† Dignity, in whatever way we understand it, can only lose by that self-sufficiency which affects to depend on self alone, and refuses to bow before the Gospel. "When a man has rebelled against the Gospel," says Madame Swetchine, "he has given himself a master, and that is himself; a master who prepares the way for many more by a continual descent."‡

Faith is no more opposed to the freedom of reason than to its dignity; as we have already said, it

---

* *Pensées*, tom. ii. p. 26. Paris, 1862. † *Ibid.*
‡ *Madame Swetchine: Sa Vie et ses Œuvres. Pensées*, tom. ii. p. 109. Paris, 1860.

is only contrary to the libertinism of reason. "Why," observes Madame Swetchine, "should not faith bind our understanding, as morality binds our actions? Do we cease to be free because we are virtuous? Why should we cease to be free because we are believers? Does not true liberty always exercise itself in a given space? Does it not require a centre to attract it, and a basis for its support?"*

* *De la Vérité du Christianisme*, p. 85.

CHAPTER X.

Recapitulation of the Causes of Infidelity—How a Young Man may become an Infidel.

BELIEVE that I have now pointed out the chief causes of infidelity. These causes, as I have shown, are many and diverse; but infidelity depends far more on the will and on a certain moral state of the soul, than on the understanding. Faith is an act of the understanding, since its object is the revealed truth of God; but in order that the understanding may give its assent to Divine Truth and firmly adhere to it, the intervention of the will is necessary, and under the inspiration of the grace of God, the will intervenes freely. This grace is refused to none. Faith is free; therefore it is meritorious; faith is a virtue, and virtue, as a moral act, presupposes freedom. Man is free to choose between faith and unbelief, in the same way that he is free to choose between good and evil, on condition of bearing the responsibility of his choice. We are free to adhere or not to adhere to revealed truth; first, because even in things that are evident, it depends on ourselves whether we will turn away the eyes of our understanding from the light that enlightens all

things—whether we will arrest the spring of our mind, give it a false direction or even corrupt it; secondly, because the principal object of faith is not self-evident, but is obscure. "All religion is in the same plane: light is always mingled with obscurity; and why? In order that faith may be a virtue."* This mingling of light and darkness is the necessary condition of this present life, because it is a life of probation; the full day will dawn only when trial shall have ceased.

Ignorance itself, which is one of the commonest sources of infidelity, is often the result of an evil-disposed will. In such case ignorance is culpable, and its guilt is greater or less, according as it is more or less wilful. How can we excuse the levity, the dissipation, the indifference in which most unbelievers live, and whence their ignorance of religion proceeds? Are not reasonable beings bound to seek seriously and sincerely the knowledge of the truth? Moral indifference, the ordinary source of religious ignorance, is capable of leading to every degree of degradation and ruin. When a mind is infected by it, it rarely stops at the rejection of Christianity, but almost always descends to the denial or corruption of the fundamental principles of natural religion; generally it becomes materialistic, and believes only in sensible realities. Materialism, which is the lowest degree of moral and intellectual degradation, is the most frequent

---

* Madame Swetchine, *Pensées*, tom. ii. p. 89.

result of indifference in religious matters. Scepticism, which is the supreme impotence of reason, often depends on a moral condition similar to that which engenders and nourishes materialism. In certain minds of high intelligence, eager for truth, it may spring from a senseless pride which has had a cruel fall. People flatter themselves that they can remove the limits of reason; they want to be able to see the truth without clouds, and when these clouds, which they believed themselves able to disperse, continually reappear, they grow angry, and end by denying the light because of the shadows which they themselves cast upon it. This is the despair of disappointed pride. But there is a malady of the soul still more difficult to cure than scepticism or materialism, and it is that condition of intellectual corruption which is called sophistry. We have seen this frightful and fatal malady, which destroys many highly-gifted minds. It is useless to seek to convince sophists that they are in error; they will not understand you; they contradict themselves at every step, whilst they maintain with imperturbable assurance that they never contradict themselves, and that they constantly obey reason. They are minds which literally see everything crosswise, and it is impossible to reason with them. "If thy eye be clear," says the Gospel, "thy whole body shall be lightsome; but if thy eye be evil, thy whole body shall be darksome."* The intellectual eye of

* Matt. vi. 22, 23.

sophists is evil; simplicity and clearness must be restored to it, otherwise they cannot receive the light, or they receive it imperfectly. How can this be done? Only by changing the soul in its inmost depths. Let them yield less to egotism; let them love truth more; let their will be simple and just, and their understanding will promptly recover that uprightness which is the condition of true enlightenment.

The greatest obstacle to the Christian Faith is egotism; egotism of the senses, or sensuality; egotism of the mind, or pride; egotism in every form. We have each of us daily to struggle against this egotism, which shuts out innumerable souls from the light of Faith. If unbelievers, of whatever kind, were animated by a generous love of truth—if they showed that they were ready to embrace it at the price of any sacrifice—they would soon become Christians. Their will, recovering its rectitude and its moral energy, would turn the eye of the understanding in the right direction, and would confirm the understanding in its adhesion to recognized truth. Doubtless we may hesitate even in the face of known truth; but such hesitation is a culpable weakness, and if the will be pure and vigorous it will not hesitate. Moreover, God will sustain it, because it will be humble and suppliant as it becomes every created will to be.

See this young man of twenty. He has been baptized into the Church of God, and has received the Divine seed of Faith in the Sacrament of regeneration. This blessed seed has germinated under the breath of the Holy Spirit, and by the culture which it has received from the pious solicitude of a Christian family. This young man has made his first Communion, he has been marked in the Sacrament of Confirmation with the seal of Christian manhood. But now he believes no longer; the Christian life of his soul has disappeared; Faith appears to be wholly extinct within him. He goes so far as even to affect pity for the belief which in his tender years he shared with his mother; he parades a supreme contempt for the teaching of the Church of Jesus Christ; he is astonished that defenders of such teaching can still be found; he is inclined to regard the defenders of the Faith of his childhood as hypocrites, seeking to make their profit out of the ignorance and credulity of the simple. What can have happened to work such a revolution in this youthful mind? If we ask him, he will probably tell us what are the new sources of light whence he has drawn decisive proofs against that old Faith which for nineteen centuries has held captive the loftiest intellects, and reigned over the noblest and the purest wills. What has this contemptuous youth seen of the Faith of Bossuet, of Leibnitz, of Joseph Görres, of Lacordaire, of Ozanam, of so many eminent men who in our days have adorned and still adorn philosophy, literature, criticism, science? Hear him: he has scrutinized everything, examined everything by the torch of pure and independent reason. The Catholic Creed cannot sustain for a moment the examination of serious criticism. Philosophy, history, science, agree to condemn it. . . . What composure! what assurance! what proud, triumphant judgments! But these lofty affirmations, these pompous maxims, cannot impose on any one who has had experience of men and things; such an one easily discovers behind this clatter of pretensions and empty phrases the true history of this poor soul. It is this:

This young man, who so proudly condemns Catholic belief, has examined nothing for himself; he has had neither the leisure nor the will to do so. He has read none of the great works of the Christian apologists; he has not even opened a detailed and scientific exposition of the dogmas which the Church teaches. He condemns Christianity on hearsay with the lightest and blindest faith that can be imagined. His morals being already tainted, doubt entered his soul the first time he heard a contemptuous word spoken with regard to the Faith which had enlightened his tender years; he gave ear to the word of the tempter, which met with a sympathetic and ready echo in a heart already degraded, or on the eve of becoming so. Doubt having penetrated his soul and disturbed its serenity, he sought not to conquer it; on the contrary, he acted so as to encourage it and with the secret desire of beholding its perfect triumph over the ruins of an austere faith. He let loose his sensual passions, or at least contenting himself with avoiding gross excess, he did but half restrain them; he fed his understanding with writings hostile to Catholicism, and would only read such books and journals as calumniated the Church in her dogma, her worship, her history, her present life, in all her manifestations. These writings, in which ignorance rivals hate, are henceforth his sole light, his sole authority in religious questions; he blindly repeats the sentences he finds in them, imagining perhaps that he is judging the teaching of Faith with entire intellectual independence. Poor young man! Your affected independence of reason will only deceive children; any serious observer will tell you how you have descended all the steps of the ladder of doubt and infidelity; he will give you the history of your moral and intellectual falls, and placing his finger on the wounds of your heart, as well as on the wounds of your understanding, he will force you to confess, if you are sincere, that reason and science have no part in your condition, and that your unbelief is the fruit of weakness and decay of every kind. Do not deceive yourself; infidelity is not an elevation, but a degradation; it is a fall, it is a moral and intellectual decline; and this decline in a young man who has been educated in the Christian Faith is usually brought about by the ruin of more faculties than one. Some young men fall into infidelity in consequence of manifold low and degrading actions, which have extinguished their moral life. Many, thank God, descend not thus far; they stop themselves on the sad incline. They lose the Faith by hostile teaching, by irreligious reading, by intercourse with indifferent or adverse companions, by the very atmosphere of infidelity that surrounds them; but though their soul may have undergone many falls, the moral life still animates it. La Bruyère said: "I would fain see a man who is sober, moderate, chaste, equitable, declare that there is no God; he would at least speak disinterestedly; but such a man is not to be found."* For my part, I would fain see a young man who is chaste, modest, humble, seriously instructed in Christian doctrine, declare, that the Faith which he received from his mother the Catholic Church is without foundation: hitherto I have never met with such a young man.

But what I have often seen, what we see every day, is this: men of ripe intellect, after years of wandering, return to the Faith and to the practices which it imposes, acknowledging and declaring, in all humility, that their unbelief was but the fruit of vanity, ignorance, or passion. It is a fact of daily observation that men regain the summits of faith by the pure and persevering love of truth and virtue, as they descend into the abyss of infidelity by

* *Les Caractères*, chap. xvi., "Des Esprits Forts."

pursuing a contrary path. A pure and humble soul, loving truth and justice, opens of itself to the light of faith ; and the holier it is, the higher in the moral order, the greater its knowledge of God and of itself, the deeper and more lively will be its faith. Faith grows in direct proportion to the purity and moral light of the soul. This is a fact attested by the whole history of Christianity. I will conclude by recommending this fact to the consideration of all sincere men.

FINIS.

www.ingramcontent.com/pod-product-compliance
Lightning Source LLC
Chambersburg PA
CBHW031730230426
43669CB00007B/306